Life & Death on the
Loxahatchee

To Betty, with
best wishes

Jim Snyder

Life and Death on the Loxahatchee : The Story of Trapper Nelson
by James D. Snyder.

© 2002 by James D. Snyder. All rights reserved.
Published by Pharos Books, 8657 SE Merritt Way, Jupiter, FL 33458-1007

Cover and interior design and production by Pneuma Books
Set in Bulmer MT 12.5/15

Cover Illustration: Painting ©Ron Parvu; Tequesta, Florida. See page 149.

First Printing. First Edition. Printed in the United States of America
11 10 09 08 07 06 05 04 03 02   1 2 3 4 5 6 7 8 9 10 11

LCCN 2002190070

Other books by James D. Snyder:

*All God's Children: How the First Christians Challenged the Roman World and
Shaped the Next 2000 Years — The Tumultuous Story of AD 31-71*
(1999, 680 pp., ISBN 0-9675200-0-2)

*The Faith and the Power: The Inspiring Story of the First Christians and How
They Survived the Madness of Rome — A First Century History*
(2002, 416 pp. ISBN 0-9675200-2-9)

These, and *Life and Death on the Loxahatchee*, are available at bookstores, through
National Book Network at 800/462-6420, and online via amazon.com and
barnesandnoble.com.

Publisher's Cataloging-in-Publication
(Provided by Quality Books, Inc.)

Snyder, James D.
   Life and death on the Loxahatchee : the story of
Trapper Nelson / James D. Snyder. -- 1st ed.
   p. cm.
   Includes bibliographical references.
   ISBN 0-9675200-3-7

   1. Nelson, Trapper. 2. Zoo keepers--Florida--
Biography. 3. Trapper Nelson's Zoo and Jungle Garden.
4. Jupiter (Fla.)--Biography.   I. Title.

QL31.N45S69 2002   590'.7'3092
                                QBI02-701380

Life & Death on the
Loxahatchee

The Story of Trapper Nelson

James D. Snyder

Pharos
Books

To Kyle, Melinda, Jessica and Rachel.
I hope this will help you keep the Loxahatchee
and its story alive for your grandchildren as well.

Acknowledgments

This book is a tribute in part to a unique group of people, who still stay in touch and still celebrate their common heritage at yearly Pioneers of Jupiter reunions. Most are in their eighties or nineties as this is written, but there isn't one among them who isn't sharp of tongue and memory. For offering their friendship to and sharing their experiences with an outsider who has lived on the Loxahatchee only ten years, I thank Dave and Agnes Brooker, Carroll Little Dorsey, Louis and Margie Freeman, Dodie DuBois Hawthorne, Wilson Horne, Ruby Fortner Lanier, Beau Mayo, Jim Minear, Roy and Patricia Rood and Carlin White. My salute embraces such latter generation collaborators as Eric Bailey, John R. DuBois III, Nathaniel P. Reed, Sylvia Pennock and her daughter Ramona Pennock Stark.

Others contributed in many ways. My wife Sue, as always, was the first to blow the whistle on shoddy workmanship. Bob Schuh, a Jonathan Dickinson State Park ranger, read the manuscript with an eye for accurately depicting Trapper Nelson's camp. Patricia Magrogan did so because she's president of Friends of the Loxahatchee and has lived here for forty-plus years. Her neighbor Bill Wood, an attorney and local historian, lent the same critical eye. Fourteen-year-old Melinda Shepherd (my very smart granddaughter) critiqued the story's appeal to young people. Others invaluable to this project were Milda Enos, local bookstore proprietor and painstaking proofreader; Richard Procyk, a homicide detective-turned-archeologist; Catherine Dosa, friend and Florida History Museum docent; Brian Taylor, my ever-patient book designer; and artist Ron Parvu, Jupiter's own incarnation of Andrew Wyeth (see cover and page 149).

Most of all, I'd like to thank the few family members of Trapper Nelson I have been fortunate to know. They are Lucille Celmer (the wife of his sister's son), Philip Celmer III (her son) and Marcie Celmer (Phil's daughter). During our interviews it was obvious that they loved Vince Nelson and revered his memory. Despite some initial misgivings that an outsider might try to invent a tawdry tale, they gave me the freedom and the family records necessary to present Trapper Nelson as I saw him — warts and all.

To Lucille, Phil and Marcie, I hope you find your trust has been justified.

JDS

Preface

Four times a day the aluminum pontoon boat *Loxahatchee Queen II* churns its way up the river with sightseers from the 11,000-acre Jonathan Dickinson State Park just northwest of Jupiter, Florida. Its destination on the 45-minute ride upstream is the park's centerpiece, the restored compound once occupied for more than 35 years by Vince "Trapper" Nelson.

Of course the best way to go is the way Trapper did back in 1933. Paddle a canoe up Florida's only federally designated Wild and Scenic River and you've soon left all visible civilization behind. At first the Loxahatchee is brackish, a hundred feet and more wide, with tall mangroves leaning over the sloping banks. In a mile or so the river narrows and begins to curl like a snake's crawl. Saltwater intrusion from the Atlantic Ocean six miles eastward now wanes and gives way to a freshwater ecology. Large ferns, saw palmettos, pond apple trees and stunted maples are joined by battered old cypress trees that form the retreating rear guard against the continued saltwater invasion. As the river depth declines, you see catfish and mullet wiggling over the sandy bottom in the tannin-stained water. Turtles sun on fallen logs, herons stand motionless on the shore as they stay focused on the serious business of spearfishing. Overhead, an osprey vectors in on a fish from a dead cypress branch and turkey buzzards hover higher up in the constant breeze.

After another mile your arms start to ache a bit. The current against you is stronger because you're that much closer to its powerful aquifer source, the Loxahatchee Slough. At this point the river is but thirty or so feet across and you'll scrape bottom if you don't stay in the meandering channel. Hyacinth begins to clog your way in spot, and little rivulets beckon like sirens wanting to lure you to a dead-end marsh — and perhaps home to one of the park's sixty or so gators.

Then just as you round another identical bend you're staring squarely at a hundred feet of boat dock, all hewn together from "fat-lighted" pine logs (so full of natural turpentine when they were cut that they still ward off worms and rot). Most of the dock is topped with a crude, corrugated metal roof.

Welcome to the remains of Trapper Nelson's Zoo and Jungle Garden. As you stride past abandoned animal cages or stop at a tin-roofed chickee hut that now serves as a picnic area, the only sounds may be the faint hum from Interstate 95 and the Florida Turnpike, the aorta of Southeast Florida's three million residents and a million more tourists.

Vince Nelson picked this place to live the rest of his life until his mysterious death in 1968. In fact, "mysterious," — or better, "mystique" — are words that followed him all his life. Perhaps it's because he was so much like his beloved Loxahatchee. Both have many dimensions. Neither has allowed anyone to peer deep within them. And each has remained a symbol of the last stubborn resistance to the relentless incursion of asphalt, concrete and cable that advances on South Florida each day.

Above all, Trapper Nelson was a man who lived life on his own terms. This is his story — and, of course, the drastically different world of early Jupiter.

Natulkiewicz

I

1908 – 32

"**W**ake up, Charlie, John! Have a look at this!" The freight train was rolling to a near stop, probably to pick up a load of logs on its way south to Miami. Vince Nelson had been squinting through a slight opening in the sliding door of their boxcar, and now he rolled it wide open with a bold shove so the other two stowaways could see what he'd been gawking at.

The early morning sun streamed into the boxcar as the train barely crawled over a low bridge across a river maybe a football field wide. Below them an incoming tide had brought in a swift current the color of aquamarine. Their mouths hung open as they studied mounds of live oyster beds, then deep pools of clear water with the slender tops of large fish stacked like cordwood against the bridge's wooden pilings. Every few seconds the surface would break with the leap of a frisky fish that they would soon come to know intimately as mullet. On the north side of the river was a handsome red lighthouse and a few outbuildings. On the south or right shore were several docks and frame houses sitting behind a shallow sand beach. Well beyond them to the east they could make out silent whitecaps surging in from the Atlantic Ocean.

In a few minutes they could feel the train start to lurch forward again. It was time for a quick decision. "Who needs to go to Miami?" boomed Vince. "Look at all that land and water. You'll never go hungry living in this place." As soon as the train reached the other side of the bridge, the three young adventurers from Trenton, New Jersey had swung to the ground with their bags of clothes, knives, guns and trapping gear.

At age 23, Vince had already ridden the rails so long that he didn't think twice about walking atop a freight train swaying along at sixty miles an hour. He was already an experienced trapper, tanner and hunter. Today "survivalist" usually means someone who keeps a gun and tins of C-rations in his basement. In 1931 Vince was a seasoned survivalist in the acute sense that he had faced starvation with no money in his pockets. And now, as Depression gripped the nation some two years after the worst stock market crash in history, others were learning what it meant as well.

He was born Vincent Natulkiewicz in Trenton on November 6, 1908,1 the second youngest of five children. The name and family were a mixture of Polish and Russian. His father had come to America in 1903 and had found a job in a ceramics factory. He spoke only Polish, and when Vince was a child he would accompany his father shopping to make sure local merchants didn't get the best of him. In fact, Vince was a very bright lad who excelled in mathematics when he graduated from eighth grade.

But there the formal education stopped — perhaps because it was also about that time that the family itself began to unravel. Vince's mother had died when he was 13. When his father remarried, Vince and his older brother Charlie couldn't accept their new stepmother. They had already spent long summer days trapping groundhogs because the state paid a bounty on them. Then they'd trapped muskrats and otters around Lake Carnegie outside of Trenton. Soon the days away from home stretched into fall and winter.

At age 17 or 18, Vince Natulkiewicz got a job on a road gang building the Pulaski Skyway in New Jersey. It paid 50 cents an hour, and he wouldn't have liked it had it paid ten times that much. Something else added to his misery. He had leapt from adolescence into the world of romance by falling in love with a married woman. When she ended the affair — whether torrid or tranquil isn't known — by announcing that she was going back to her husband, the young man was crushed. "That was the day he also smashed up the family car," his sister Marcie would say.

Soon afterward, Vince, his best friend John Dykas, and his brother Charlie — eight years his senior — were off to see the U.S.A., relying on the rail system with thousands of other hobos and job seekers. By the time they reached Colorado, they'd already trapped along the way, selling hides and shooting craps in boxcars for enough cash to stay alive. They rode the rails all the way to southernmost Texas. One day, after they'd wandered across the Rio Grande to the Mexican side, Vince was setting traps when he looked up to find himself surrounded by Federales. The Mexican civil war was raging and the government troops thought the husky young American was probably running guns across the river to Zapata and his rebels.

So it was several weeks in a rat-infested, adobe Mexican prison while the authorities pondered what to do with him. They had no firm evidence, but what they did know was that the prisoner was eating so much they couldn't afford to keep him. By then young Vince had filled out to 220 pounds on a barrel-chested, six-foot-two frame.

He also had deep blue eyes and movie star looks. Once released from jail, Vince hopped aboard another freight train headed for California, but Hollywood wasn't exactly waiting at the other end. After setting traps for weeks in the unfriendly, unproductive Mohave Desert, he found himself penniless and near starvation. Years later he would tell friends in Jupiter that he might have died if he hadn't stumbled into an orange grove. "The oranges were huge, almost like melons, and they tasted awfully sour, but they saved my life," he would say. It was some time before he realized that he'd been gorging on grapefruits.

It was back to Trenton for a rendezvous with Charlie and John, but all three soon got the travel itch again once they compared the snow and ice of the New Jersey winter with what they'd sampled in sunnier climes. This time they decided to head southeast for, maybe West Palm Beach, maybe the Everglades or even the Florida Keys. The Jupiter that the trapper trio landed upon in September 1931 consisted of about 250 souls, and only if you counted the little knot of Afro-American families that had their own close-knit community further to the west. Three years before, a landmark hurricane — the kind where everyone remembers just what they were doing the night it struck — had battered the little wooden homes, and people were just now completing the long rebuilding process.

But the essence of Jupiter and its "first families" were still there. Anchoring the town just off the ocean inlet was the fish camp, boat dock and restaurant run by John and Bessie DuBois. Behind them on Jupiter's only hill was the old frame home built in 1898 by John's parents, Harry and Susan DuBois, when they were newlyweds. The "hill" was actually the same Indian shell mound that Jonathan Dickinson

and his family found in 1696 when they were shipwrecked
in a hurricane and captured by the hostile Jeaga (sometimes
called Hobe) Indians before beginning a harrowing north-
ward journey that led to their rescue by the Spanish at St.
Augustine several months later.

Dickinson's journal recorded the ease with which his cap-
turers were able to spear and scoop fish from the inlet to feed
the village each night. Snook, tarpon, sea trout, mutton snapper, mackerel, pompano, giant jewfish, oysters, blue crabs —
all still teemed in the waters around the DuBois fish camp,
and wealthy sport fishermen helped make it the hub of Jupiter
life. The DuBois dock was also where the School Boat came
to pick up and drop off kids from across the river who at-
tended Jupiter's school house near the railroad tracks on Old
Dixie Highway.

If Jupiter had an "industry" at the time, it was probably the
growing of asparagus ferns for commercial nurseries up north.
In fact, the same Miami-bound train the young trappers jumped
from would probably stop on its return trip to load crates of
ferns so that florists up north would have a nice green backdrop when they prepared their bouquets. A mile or so upriver
families cultivated ferns on five to ten acre plots that now fetch
a million dollars an acre. Best known among them was Pennock Plantation (also a dairy and nursery serving the West
Palm Beach market), which provided Depression-era jobs for
many families that would eventually make their marks in other
ways. Amos Bassett ran the fernery, Lloyd Minear the dairy
and Harry Jackson the company finances. Families like the
Roods and Wilkinsons all worked first at Pennock Plantation
before saving enough to start their own businesses.

Others had their own homegrown, hardscrabble enter-
prises. Kenneth Horne raised chickens and cows when he

wasn't being school janitor. The Bowers ran the general store and traded with Seminole Indians for some of their goods. The Carlins, who boasted of having Jupiter's oldest house (circa 1889) rented guest cabins and looked after the Western Union outpost. John and Bessie DuBois took in boarders along with running a fish camp and restaurant. The Youngs raised tomatoes, beans, peppers, potatoes and onions. Across the river, the Seabrooks took care of the lighthouse. Ray Roebuck moved up from West Palm Beach to become the area's only lawyer.

The three trappers slipped into town without much notice, just as scores of drifters and campers did on their way up and down Florida's east coast in search of elusive jobs. It was also about this time that the two Natulkiewicz brothers decided that a new start in life deserved a new surname. It would now be Nelson — and for no other reason than that it was easier on the ears. As Vince would later explain, "It just seemed to me that if people have a hard time pronouncing your name, you ought to do something to make it easier for them."

"Home" in Jupiter was a crude hunting-trapping camp in a largely uninhabited hammock just south of the Inlet and near the weather-beaten town beach pavilion. One day it would become Carlin Beach Park and the Ocean Dunes condominiums, but then it was just a stretch of wind-bent scrub pines a few yards behind the dune line. The squatters bored a well and set up a crude lean-to. " I can remember seeing their animal skins hanging from boards," recalls Dodie Hawthorn, a daughter of John and Bessie DuBois.

The DuBois family saw a lot of Vince in the early months because their fish camp was the nearest destination when he would cross the Intracoastal to the mainland. Grandson John DuBois III, who became president of the Florida History

Center and Museum in 2000, recalls that many of his grandmother's favorite stories centered on the young man from Trenton and his soon-to-be-legendary appetite. "At one point she and my grandfather were boarding a small, prim man who was involved in running the wireless machine for the lighthouse across the river," he says. "One night this scrawny fellow and the very muscular Vince were eating dinner at the same table. When they asked what was for dessert, my grandmother brought out a large lemon meringue pie. The little guy sliced off a sliver. Vince's piece was the rest of the pie."

Trapping by the beach may have been profitable — enough to garner a few hundred dollars and buy an old car — but pleasant it was not. According to Charlie Nelson, Dykas wasn't much of a trapper to begin with, yet wanted to be paid a full one-third of what they got from selling pelts to wholesalers. Worse yet, it seemed that Dykas was coming between him and his little brother — the kid he'd taught to trap and had looked after through all their scrapes and travails out west.

On December 17, 1931, John DuBois, who also served as Jupiter's seldom-used constable for the West Palm Beach police, was ordered by phone to go to down to the trapper's camp and watch over a dead body until detectives could arrive to begin an inquiry.

What happened? Charlie Nelson had driven the old car 15 miles to the West Palm police station, parked it right in front with a shotgun lying on the back seat, and matter-of-factly told the desk sergeant that he'd just shot a trapper named John Dykas. Hit him right between the eyes with his shotgun. Killed him instantly.

Why? According to Charlie's written confession, it happened around 8:30 that morning while Vince had been off checking his traps. Dykas was sitting on an upended wooden crate holding a fork and stirring a pan full of pancakes and grits. Charlie came out of the lean-to, stretched, and announced that he'd decided to strike out on his own. Somehow Dykas had become camp treasurer and held all the money they'd gotten from selling pelts up north. Charlie asked for "my share of the business" right then and there.

Dykas thought about it and agreed, but he wouldn't give Charlie more than $50.

"Finally I'd just had enough," Charlie told the detectives. "So this morning I told Dykas he had 15 minutes to give me my fair share or I was going to kill him."

When Dykas continued to stir his skillet in silence, Charlie walked inside the lean-to, emerged with his shotgun and announced that the time was up. One of the twin barrels hadn't worked for years, but Charlie fired the good one.

If John Dykas could have taken the witness stand, he might have said something like this: Charlie Nelson was a wild and free spirit — sometimes too much so for his own good. He'd already been arrested for drunken driving back in Trenton and had continued his boozing in Jupiter. He boasted too much, talked too loudly and acted like a big boss when he should have shown a man a little respect.

In any event, the murder of John Dykas was big news all the way from Palm Beach to Stuart. Both Nelson brothers were jailed. When Charlie surprised everyone by inexplicably pleading not guilty, a first-degree murder trial was set for January 20, 1932. As circuit court judge Curtis E. Chillingworth began interviewing 43 candidates for a jury, Vince was released on a $500 bond. Charlie went on being Charlie, quickly becoming top dog in the jailhouse and deciding who slept where and who did what chores.

He also became news fodder for the *Palm Beach Post*, whose reporters seemed to have easy access for interviews. Looking jaunty in hunting boots, knee breeches and a sporty khaki shirt, he told a reporter, "When I go to the stand, I may say nothing and I may say anything." Yes, he regretted what he'd done, "but what good does it do to cry about it?" In fact, Charlie's biggest worry seemed to be running out of roll-your-own smokes. As the *Post* of January 7 told it:

> *Just before going back to [his jail cell] Nelson called a reporter over and thrust a $1 bill into his hand.*
>
> *"Go to the store and get me some more of that R.J.R. tobacco, will you buddy?" he said. "Go to a grocery and get me one of them big one-pound packages. They cost 40 cents."*
>
> *He refused to let the reporter stand treat.*
>
> *"Be a sport and take the money," he said.*
>
> *"You know, I think he's happier than I am," remarked Jailer T. P. Riggs in court this morning with an expression of wonder on his face.*[2]

The first trial date came and went because the court couldn't find two material witnesses. Two hunters (also from Trenton) had been tenting not far from the Nelson-Dykas camp and they'd come running when they heard the shotgun blast. But both had since gone off hunting in the Everglades on the assumption that Charlie's own confession had made their court testimony unnecessary.

In time, sheriff's deputies produced the witnesses. Then

came delay number two. The day before the trial a U.S. immigration inspector showed up to demand that Charlie face deportation charges on grounds that when he was four years old in 1904, he and his parents had been illegally smuggled into the United States from Vilna, Poland (recently annexed from Russia). Charlie was quick to swear it the truth, but the judge found the whole scene a bit too contrived or coincidental.

The trial finally began in early February. Until then the only testimony against Charlie — aside from his prior confession — was that of his own brother. Vince had calmly stated that Dykas, in fact, *had* done his share of the work and that it was Charlie who constantly baited him. But Vince had always told John Dykas never to let himself get sucked into an argument with Charlie.

Now taking the stand as the sole witness in his defense, Charlie Nelson began answering his court-appointed attorney's line of questions the way they'd rehearsed it. But in the middle of it his voice broke off and tears began flowing. No, it hadn't been he who had wanted to leave, he said between sobs. The night before, Vince — the kid he'd practically raised — had told him it was time to clear out. He offered $75 and the car if Charlie would just get his belongings and drive off the next morning. Charlie'd been struck dumb with shock, but in the end he nodded his agreement.

He got up very early the next day and went off bluefish fishing in the surf. Before he did, he told Vince that he'd changed his mind about leaving. When he returned, Dykas was cooking pancakes in a skillet over a campfire while he and Vince "huddled about something."

"I held out a plate for my share of the breakfast," he said," but Vince said 'No, this isn't for you. That's yours over there.'"

That little slight probably hurt more than anything. After breakfast, Vince went off into the hammock to check his trap line. Charlie went out to start the car, which was having battery trouble, then sat in the front seat reading a detective story while the engine revved up. After several minutes he went back to the camp for a drink of water. Dykas, who was cleaning up, looked up and said softly, "You know, Charlie, your brother really wants you to leave."

Charlie thought about it. "Okay," he said at last, but he wanted a third of the money right then and there. Dykas didn't answer. Charlie sat boiling in his own anger. What the hell did these guys want anyway? At this point the stories again coincide. He told John Dykas that he'd give him 15 minutes to hand over his fair share or he'd kill him.

The next thing he knew, the sobbing Charlie testified, "I felt the gun kick me and I glanced over and seen him laying there. I seen what a predicament I was in, so I just decided the best thing I could do was come in and give up."

Had he ever had a memory lapse? asked his public defender attorney. Yes, said Charlie. A year or so before he'd been hit by a car in California and had lain unconscious in a hospital for several days.

This gave the defense attorney at least a small thread to begin weaving a plea. To this he stitched in an appeal that "this stupid, honest trapper had become overcome with grief at the prospect of losing his brother and pal." It was enough to make the jury spare Charlie electrocution by the state's infamous "Old Sparky." On February 16, 1932, Judge Chillingworth sentenced Charles Nelson to life in Raiford Prison, just a few miles from the Georgia border.

Before he was taken away, Charlie's temper had replaced his tears. He turned around facing Vince and vowed before the courtroom to come back and kill him. Then he turned pointed at Judge Chillingworth and made the same threat.

Vince had told the painful truth, had done the right thing. But he was also 24, alone, and broke again after paying the bail bondsman. In the winter of '32 all he knew is that he didn't want to go back to icy Trenton. With game getting "trapped out" on the south side of Jupiter Inlet, he moved to the north side and pitched camp near where Perry Como later built a house on what is now the village of Jupiter Inlet Colony. For awhile he tried partnering with an irascible fellow known now only as "The Scotsman." When Vince finally had enough of his complaining, he told him to leave.

"Why me?" griped the Scotsman. "Why don't *you* leave?"

"Because I'm bigger than you," answered Vince. At a time when anyone six-foot-two and 220 pounds might have been the biggest guy on a college football team, Trapper Vince Nelson was already getting a reputation for being stronger and tougher than anyone else in Jupiter.

However, it didn't help him battle the weather. In the summer of '33 a cloudburst began around 5 P.M. and didn't stop until the next day after 18 inches of rain had fallen. The Inlet was barely open at the time and the water was trapped inside the Loxahatchee and Indian rivers. "You could row a boat anywhere in town," recalled Jim Basset. Up at Pennock Plantation "we had to jack the cows up to milk them," the dairy manager quipped, and Jack Horne remembered that "all our chickens drowned because they were so dumb they automatically jumped down from their perches when daylight came."

The floods drained in time, but it may have been the deciding factor that caused Vince Nelson to make the most important decision of his life. He'd become a squatter upriver, far enough so that news reporters couldn't follow him and wild enough that he'd never run out of game to trap, shoot, net or hook.

This meant a different ecology as well. The Loxahatchee known by Jupiter townsfolk was an extension of the ocean (at least when nature left the Inlet open). It was salty, sandy or grassy on the bottom, and nearly a mile wide in places. The river Nelson would travel with his guns and traps took on a much different personality around five miles west of the Intracoastal Waterway. There the main channel began to break up into fingers of India tea. Another two miles west lay the entrance to narrow Kitching Creek, lined with brooding centuries-old cypress trees.

Now the meandering fingers could become a dangerous gamble for any traveler — especially at night — because some wound past islands and some wound up in ankle-deep mangrove swamps. It hadn't changed much since 1923 when Harold C. Rolls wrote an article for the *Palm Beach Post* about a trip he'd taken on a motorboat owned by Frank Shuflin, one of Jupiter's first tour guides.

> *Every bend brings an exclamation of surprise.*
> *We are getting above the brackish water line now*
> *and the growth is changing. Cypress, palms of*
> *all descriptions, including a species resembling*
> *the Washingtonia which Shuflin says is rare and*
> *soft maple in two colors — green and red — make*
> *a background for all sorts of growth.*
> *The late summer green of the coastal vegeta-*

*tion has disappeared and a fresh green, re-
mindful of an April up north, replaces it. Some
of the maple leaves turned into an autumn red
and another one just coming out in a fresh yellow green a few feet away, makes a huge natural bouquet. Spanish moss is everywhere. It fes-
toons high trees and hangs from the boughs from
which the cypress reach out across narrow channels. On the trees are air plants with a reddish
bloom and wild orchids. The vegetation is so thick
and the scene so wild that it seems we are on the
Congo instead of the Loxahatchee.*

*At every turn the river becomes more gorgeous
until the pilot announces that we are just now
beginning to get into the beautiful part of the
stream. We are running now through a dark
channel of not 50 feet wide and which we learn
is 40 to 50 feet deep [locals remember nothing
more than eight to ten feet deep]. Turtles plunge
before our boat and ahead Shuflin spots a big
gator sliding into the river....*

*We have left the last vestige of civilization behind
now and the only mark of man's coming in the
whole country along the stream from now on is
a single hut — an old deserted fishing camp. Here
we stop to snap an oddity — two trees grafted together by the wind — the dark and the white wood
growing together in each other's embrace.*

*We have traveled for several hours and must
be 20 miles up. We hardly believe Shuflin when
he says that we are only a few miles from the At-*

> *lantic, so badly have the crooks and bends of the*
> *river deceived us. From here on the journey must*
> *be made by canoe as the channel becomes more*
> *and more tortuous, and reluctantly we back out*
> *into the stream and point the boat nose about.*[3]

The last place a motorboat could go before turning around is also the site Vince Nelson picked. Upstream the river's current quickened as the ribbon-like channels narrowed — many of them only five or six feet wide. Cypress knees stuck out on both shores like brown tenpins and overhead the cypress canopy was thick enough to block out the sun on the brightest day. Just southwest above that stretch, the most furious battle of the Seminole Indian War had been fought about a hundred years before. But the last bend just before all that offered a gradual slope to the water from land partially cleared by some long-forgotten squatter.

Vince Nelson, nearing his 25th birthday, had committed himself so firmly to this new world that he would quickly undergo another name change. For the rest of his life he'd be known simply as "Trapper Nelson."

Depression?

1933 – 40

Just about everyone who lived in Jupiter in the thirties invariably mentions that nobody locked their doors or even had keys. "If you dropped your wallet at the post office, it would be there at the desk when you came back," said one.

Then again, there wasn't a whole lot to steal in houses, nor much money in wallets. The Depression had sunk in like a tropical torpor. The Jupiter Inlet District had been formed to keep the mouth of the Loxahatchee open to the sea, but it had no money to spend. The WPA ran some road-building projects to give some of the locals a source of income and, as Anna Minear noted, "the Salvation Army in West Palm Beach delivered many a Christmas meal to families in Jupiter."

From Fran Histed Webb: "In those days you would go down to a point and catch snapper and have no grease to fry them in. Sometimes I felt like a neighbor who said he ate so many collard greens he had to tie kerosene rags around his ankles to keep the cutworms away."

Louis Freeman's father worked at the Pennock nursery for 15 years, but there wasn't always steady work in the Depression years. Sometimes he'd cut cypress upriver and float the logs downstream to sell to the railroad for ties. Other days he might get a job clearing land, but usually he'd make more money spearing fish. "George Martin had a fish house, and he'd pay 2 cents a pound for snook," said Freeman. "Even if a man had a job he still caught and sold fish and oysters to get extra money.

"We ate manatee and sea turtle. The sea cow tasted like pork. When smoked it tasted a little like Canadian bacon. We ate sea turtle in steaks and soup. It was against the law, but we had to live."

Everyone seemed to have more than one source of income — especially kids. Lloyd Minear ran a Plantation Dairy milk route and worked after school at Al Coston's grocery store. He was happy to make 10 cents at the store, even though his dad had offered him 15 cents an hour to wash cows at Pennock Plantation.

Glynn Mayo, who would one day become chief of police, remembered that his brother Beau and he both worked paper routes, delivering all the way out to the orange groves. "We also worked at Al Coston's store, worked in the nursery at Pennock Plantation and often helped my dad shoveling shellrock to build roads."

"I suppose we were all poor growing up," says Grace Bogardus Roselli. "We just didn't know any better." All the kids knew the inside of each other's houses, and the Loxahatchee was the center of do-it-yourself fun. Jack Wilson remembered "acres" of ducks that used to settle on the river. One time he and Judson Laird were hunting ducks on the water. Their first shots startled a whole row of a dozen or so manatees, who dove for deep water like synchronized submarines. Robert Hepburn added that he always tried to shoot ducks as soon as they arrived "because if you didn't they'd soon gorge themselves on fish and spoil their taste."

Carlin White, who turned 94 as this book was underway, once met a bear on the beach while both were hunting turtle eggs. He remembers mullet "so thick they would keep us awake at night. Each time the beam of the lighthouse would pass it would startle the mullet into a cascade of splashing." Robert Hepburn adds: "Some mornings the lawns bordering the river would be covered with mullet that had jumped out of the water during the night."

Says Roy Rood, a teenager in the thirties: "Even today, mullet is my favorite eating fish. Charlie Carlin, Ben Evans and I used to smoke them in an old refrigerator with the top cut out. We'd lay fish on the grilled shelves and light a fire in the bottom. Back then we didn't think we were eating so high on the hog."

Dave Brooker was able to buy a suit and class ring for his high school graduation by selling oysters from the Loxahatchee. "I sold oysters for 75 cents a quart and I could open a quart in 13 minutes." Robert A. Wilson remembers oysters "as big as six inches long — so big you'd have to cut them in several pieces before you could eat them."

Louis Freeman and his friends, wearing dive tanks and swim fins, would drop into deep water and spear one of the giant jewfish that hung out in herds as far up as Limestone Creek. Once they hooked a spear into one of the lumbering leviathans, they'd jump on its back and do an underwater rodeo imitation, taking turns as they went. No surprise that Freeman would later become a commercial fisherman.

Over on the lighthouse side of the river, the Seabrook kids and their friends would tie a rope to a bicycle, then ride the bike as fast as they could off the end of their dock, then they'd pull hard on the rope and dredge up the bike. At night they'd coast the shoreline with a fire suspended from a frame on the bow of the boat. When a curious fish would head for the boat, the boys would spear it. When it was a snook, it would fetch two or three cents a pound at Shuey's Inn and Trailer Park.

Shirley Floyd, one of the Pennock daughters, used to somersault into the river from the family dock. "We children also used washtubs for boats," she wrote later. "We'd take them out on the river and they'd maneuver surprisingly well. Across the river the Girl Scouts had a camp at Anchorage Point, where the swimming was great. Sometimes we'd hang onto a rope and let a motorboat tow us real fast. No water skis — just hanging on a rope."

But for inventive contraptions, probably no kids could equal the contraption contrived by Raymond Swanson and Harry DuBois. They found an old hot water heater and sawed the top off. Then they carved a window into it and connected it to a garden hose and a bicycle pump. "With 60 pounds of lead weight attached, it made a serviceable diving suit," Swanson wrote later. "It didn't smell too good, but it worked fine."

The abundance of nature also had its downside. Robert Hepburn remembered mosquitoes and sand flies so thick from May to October "that one couldn't breathe without strangling. On bad summer nights the best way to sleep was with a pillowcase over your head," he recalled thirty years later. Adds Roy Rood: "You'd just lie there at night and sweat. The next morning you'd take the mattress outside for an airing and hope it wouldn't rain."

Some homes even had a screened entryway for removing buggy clothes before going inside. Just about everyone relied on Bee Insect Powder. "Thirty-five cents bought five pounds at a time," said Amos Bassett. "We burned it in can lids and jar covers."

After Roy Rood turned eighty a dermatologist examined him and was surprised to find his skin free of the sun damage so common to beach-loving retirees. "I told him I could thank mosquitoes for that," says Rood. "When we worked all day long we'd wear long-sleeved shirts and a Frank Buck hat with a towel hanging down the back. If you didn't have that towel, the back of your neck would be covered with mosquitoes."

Aside from fishing and swimming in the river, Pennock Plantation was the hub of fun for Jupiter kids. Nearly all of them played or worked part-time jobs on the large dairy, fernery and nursery at one point while growing up. They played in the barns and haylofts and sometimes heisted eggs from the chickens. Recalled Louis Freeman: "Dave Floyd had a motorcycle that he'd use to pull a metal sled in the pasture with a couple of kids aboard. He would 'crack the whip' to swing the riders about, and if he wanted to increase the speed he'd pass the sled over a fresh manure pile."

After work all the young men would gather in a corner of Pennock's cow pasture and play baseball until dinner time or dark (there was no daylight saving time). Says Roy Rood: "We'd gather up dried cow pies — we called them sweet breads — and use them for bases. We also had a pile of clay that we'd gathered from out west of town and we used it to build a pitcher's mound.

"Baseball and swimming," that's what we did whenever we could," adds Rood. At a time when organized baseball remained severely segregated, the Pennock pasture always included blacks and whites. Owner Henry Pennock and sons Pete and Hank were all standouts, and the family pride was cousin Herb, who became a Hall of Fame lefthander for the Philadelphia A's. When Jupiter fielded semi-pro and Junior League baseball teams at a more manicured field behind the old town hall, Pennock Plantation sponsored the teams with uniforms and equipment. .

The Women's Club, just west of the train tracks where Lainhart and Potter's hardware supply now stands, was another social center, with dances, local talent nights and week-long traveling Chautauqua shows. Then there were square dances in the big room upstairs over Bower's Grocery, family outings at DuBois Park and Fourth of July celebrations at a big city pavilion on the beach (but no fireworks because they cost too much). At the old schoolhouse (long since torn down) a room on the second floor was outfitted for boxing, and the boys showed such zeal that they regularly produced Golden Gloves winners. On Sunday the kids would go to the ocean with their "sea sleds" — the thirties version of surfboards. And on very special days, they'd pile in someone's car and go off to West Palm Beach for movies and ice cream.

Both black and white families looked forward to visits by Seminole Indians. Recalled Abe Davis thirty years later: "Everybody got along with the Indians. We were always glad when they came because they brought huckleberries, wild hog and venison. They wore long shirts and no pants and came to spend the day talking to you. I never knew any of their names. They'd just say something like 'Indian man wants some corn.' They were real honest. If they said they'd be back next moon, they'd be back."

Just eight or nine miles upstream lay the much different world Vince Nelson had chosen. The shouts of children splashing and yelling were far behind, replaced only by the intermittent splash of a snook or the bellow of a surfacing manatee. And because this was not a jungle with noisy parrots or monkeys, the most frequent overhead sound was the occasional *cr-a-a-a-k* of the heron in flight and the *pee-peep pee-peep* of an osprey calling to its mate from a treetop perch. The most constant sound was the rustle of palm fronds in the tropical breeze.

It was evident from his first actions that 25-year-old Trapper Nelson intended to stay for quite some time. He planted trees: mango, orange, grapefruit, lemon, key lime, Java plum and Surinam cherry. Around these he planted rows of pineapples, then vines that, when blooming, would fill the evenings with the scent of jasmine. Finally, he cleared parts of the waterfront and planted bamboo. Over three decades, the green shoots would sprout up to sixty feet tall, breaking the mangrove-fern shoreline and announcing to any boat just emerging from around the bend that it had arrived at Trapper Nelson's compound.

Every day he set about his cash-earning business, hiking into the thicket of saw palmetto to set and inspect traps. Often he'd wear gunny sacks over his boots, smeared with an animal's scent, so as to mask his own smells and tracks from his quarry. Although there was no telling what might turn up in a trap, his aim was to strike a sustainable balance of raccoon, otter, and bobcat. Possum and skunk came with the territory as well and would fetch lesser amounts. Gators he would catch mainly for food at first.

Other trappers seem to have stayed with Trapper Nelson for short spells. The only one folks remember specifically was Joe Farrell, who lived at the camp and worked at a filling station in Jupiter until World War II when he enlisted in the navy. Recalls Dave Brooker: "He was short and thin and didn't say much, so they called him 'Little Trapper' or 'Little Joe,'" And it may have been Farrell the *Palm Beach Post-Times* interviewed many years later for a story about the early days. It quoted a "veteran Loxahatchee trapper" friend, who wouldn't be quoted by name, in describing how gator meat often wound up on the camp grill:

> *Well, we'd hang a possum night after night from the same branch over about a foot of water. After a while the alligator, well, he'd get accustomed to his evening meal being there, and pretty soon there comes Mr. Alligator tuckin' in his napkin and ready for chow.*
>
> *Soon as he lays his foot in that trap we pop out from behind a tree and loop a wire around his snout. Then we take off the trap, ease him into the boat and row home. And let me tell you, son, that was one hell of a ride!* [4]

Back at camp after a day's work, the carcasses were hatcheted, their sweat glands cut out, rinsed in the drinkable river water, parboiled in baking soda and cooked in a wood stove. Trapper Nelson ate everything from possum to catfish to gator meat. Louis Freeman remembers watching Trapper contentedly stirring a large pot containing a stew of wildcat, rice and onions. When friends asked if his diet included polecats and stray housecats as well, Trapper would just smile and wink.

His favorite food was gopher tortoise stew. Like many a

Jupiter homestead, Trapper had a special pen for gopher tortoises that had a concrete floor so they couldn't burrow underneath and escape. By just keeping a dish of fresh water and some green grass for the vegetarians to eat, he could keep a ready supply of fresh meat on hand. In those days people called gopher tortoise "Hoover chicken" in a snide reference to the man who was unfortunate enough to be president when the Depression hit.

Still, the trapper's main objective was pelts that could be shipped north to waiting furriers, as well as alligator hides for shoes and purses. After a winter season in which skins were dried over outdoor racks, a nice raccoon pelt would usually fetch $2.50, a seven-foot alligator $3 and a worm-free otter pelt upwards of $15. A rare animal might bring much more alive, such as the time when Trapper showed up at the Railway Express depot with a cage containing a black panther. Luther Ladner, the agent, recalled that Nelson had already made a deal to sell it to a New York zoo. "He's the only black panther ever seen in these parts," Trapper told the agent. "He's a mean cat, so don't pester him." Then he walked off.

When the train came and the porter tried to load the cage, the yellow-eyed cat spat right at him and reached out of the cage with a swipe of his claws. "The porter dropped the cage and jumped back on the train," said Ladner. "I had to load him myself."

Trapper lacked a car in the early years, so he had two ways to get to town on his weekly supply trips. One was walking six miles. "I can remember seeing him several times walking that road with two corn sacks full of groceries over his shoulder," says Ruby Fortner Lanier, who at 90-plus years still greets customers at her Lanier Nursery in old Jupiter.

The other way was to row the twisted eight or nine miles downstream to the DuBois fish camp. Heads would already be turning as Trapper tied his line to a cleat on the DuBois dock. Most likely he'd be in hunting boots and shorts. No shirt — just 220 pounds of bronzed muscle — and often with a bandana wrapped around his head. "*Tarzan*" was the rage at all the movie theaters, and it was easy to peg this blond, blue-eyed version with the same nickname.

Other heads may have turned for a different reason. As Bessie DuBois wrote much later in *The History of the Lox-ahatchee River*,

> *"Trapper skinned so many raccoons, wildcats and other game that even though he bathed and kept his [clean] outfits in a separate cabin, when dogs got downwind of him they would catch the scent of wildcat and bark themselves hoarse — which embarrassed both Trapper and the dog owners."* [5]

Roy Rood, then a teenager, remembers many Trapper arrivals because he'd often work at the DuBois site shoveling the shells from Indian mounds onto trucks headed for road projects. "I can still see him at the boathouse where they sold bait," says Rood. "After all that rowing, he'd polish off a box of Hershey bars and then wash it all down with a quart of milk.

"Now Neil DuBois [John's brother] raised honey bees," adds Rood, "and he had all these large metal cylinders of honey stacked up around the dock ready to ship out. I've seen Trapper scoop honey from a cylinder and fill up a milk bottle. He'd drink the honey in one swig and follow it with the usual quart of milk."

Sometimes he'd stay for dinner, adding to the growing legend about his appetite. And often he'd linger. A few of the Jupiter schoolteachers boarded at the DuBois camp, and frequently Trapper would help them grade math papers at night. "He was a whiz at math," Bessie remembered. It may also have been his interest in the young ladies that accounted for his scholarly demeanor. And if the attraction was mutual, "it would be easy to understand," DuBois said. "He was clean-shaven, didn't smoke, never drank and was never heard to swear around women. Yet he was also painfully awkward around the ladies."

"My grandmother always thought he was a gentleman, but not to be trifled with," adds John DuBois III.

As the Tarzan similarity began to play on people's minds, more of them would invent reasons for climbing in their motorboats and paying Trapper Nelson a curiosity call. Even more so when they found how ruggedly charming and entertaining he could be. Myla Roebuck wrote about taking her first trip upriver with Carlin White: "When we rounded the bend and approached the camp, Carlin fired a shot. It scared me, but in those days it was wise to notify Trapper of your arrival. I was impressed with his collection of wildlife. Especially the barrel filled with rattlesnakes."

The place was still rather primitive in those days. Trapper had a small cabin and an open-walled chickee hut, and which one he slept in depended on the day and weather. He chopped firewood every day for exercise and already there were the beginnings of a pile that would stretch more than 100 feet long by the day he died. He drank water straight from the river and cooked in an open pot suspended from a tripod. Everywhere he went, various dogs, raccoons and other "pets," some newly-converted from the wild, would follow him about. His favorite was a large indigo snake, which he'd have draped around his neck when he greeted visitors. Roosting wild in surrounding trees was a covey of guinea hens that would make a racket every time a visitor appeared.

Like most high school seniors, Grace Bogardus Roselli remembers a trip to Trapper's as the most exotic thing she could imagine doing on her "Skip Day." This was a hallowed tradition in which seniors enjoyed the unofficial rite of electing one day in their final spring term when they could play hooky secure in knowing that teachers and parents would manage to overlook their absence.

Not long after he graduated, Dave Brooker would become a charter boat captain and haul sightseers to Trapper Nelson's several times a week. But in 1937 he was just a kid with an old Model T Ford. Recalls Grace Roselli: "On Skip Day a bunch of us piled into Dave's Model T in the schoolyard. Mr. Green the principal just looked up at the noise, then just waved us off."

They headed west up a crude sandy road that led into Trapper's. "We didn't have much, so we made our own fun when we got there," says Roselli. "He had a big rope hanging from a tree by the water and we'd swing it out and dive off into the river. We never thought about snakes or gators, which were all over the place. If you got thirsty, you just dove down deep and took a gulp of water.

"I remember Trapper as a very likeable guy with a dry sense of humor," adds Roselli. "He'd let you do what you wanted, but if you were about to do something that might cause an injury, he wouldn't hesitate to tell you about it."

John R. DuBois III cites another episode that also shows the high regard his grandparents had for Trapper Nelson. "In the mid-thirties my grandmother's dad, John Wilson, had just died in a house fire. Instead of subjecting their young children to the stress of a funeral, their father sent them up to Trapper's and billed it as a special gala event. And Trapper played his role to the fullest, showing them various animals and how he trapped."

Perhaps he was realizing he had a special flair for playing Tarzan and entertaining strangers, because the idea of opening some sort of jungle attraction was already playing in his head. After all, who knew how long cash would continue to show up in traps?

The concept gained momentum when one of the local fishing boat operators down in Jupiter began appearing with tourists on board. Frank Lechleitner had arrived from Alberta, Canada, in the early thirties and by 1937 owned a boat named *Nine Bells*. It seated thirty with a wooden sunroof and, unlike most other boat guides, "Captain Frank" mostly took folks upriver. Because gasoline was too expensive for most people to make the trip in their own boats, *Nine Bells* soon attracted everyone from out-of-towners to daters to scout groups.

The climax of the trip was Trapper Nelson's, of course, and there they'd spread out their blankets and eat their picnic lunch. Louis Freeman, who "hung around whenever I could" as a teenager, remembers a kindly old Palm Beach gentleman who conducted botany tours of proper ladies from posh places like The Breakers. "As they were setting out the picnic, old Mr. Haskell asked Trapper if he would care to have a bite of lunch. Well, it consisted mostly of dainty finger sandwiches packed by the hotel staff. Trapper said that would be nice, and I started laughing to myself right away because I knew what was going to happen. I can still see him wolfing them down two or three of those little sandwiches at a time, then attacking the deviled eggs. I was there the next time Mr. Haskell brought a group, and I heard him telling the ladies on the boat to finish their lunch before they landed."

Dave Brooker, who would soon begin taking his own charter groups upriver, recalls, "when Trapper would put a leg of chicken to his teeth, you'd see the bone come clean in one swipe."

The trips upstream were often high spots in people's lives. Lillian White, who married Carlin and later wrote for the *Jupiter Courier* as well, described a moonlit trip with Captain Frank:

> *"The moon was so bright you could almost read by it, and the mullet were so plentiful they reminded me of silver sequins popping in and out of the river. We talked. We sang and some of the boys did some trolling."* [6]

Sometime around 1938 Trapper decided to take the plunge into show business. A homemade sign at his dock now read "Trapper Nelson's Jungle Zoo and Garden." And when Captain Frank arrived with his guests, there would be a little more in it for Trapper than a sandwich or three.

Now there was real work to be done. Trapper expanded on what had been just a few pens and pits for captured alligators, wildcats and other attractions. The skull from a jumbo-sized gator he'd shot in its lair a few years back was now taken out of the cabin and hung up for display. Trays of tortoise shells were now available for sale, along with pineapples and fruits from his grove. Wrapping giggly kids with an indigo snake was now part of the visitor show along with a more formal lecture on what it's like to live in the wild. Descriptions of the water were a little deeper and of the woods a bit scarier.

And often they were absolutely true. Wilson Horne remembers Trapper putting on a snake demonstration for his wide-eyed Boy Scout troop. To prove a point about treating rattlesnakes gingerly, he pointed to one of his thumbs, which was missing an inch or so just above the top joint. "See that?" he said. "One time a boy brought me a rattlesnake in a sack, and when I reached in to grab it by the neck, I missed and it bit me right there. Well, I knew the venom would start working on me long before I could get to a doctor, so...[he raised an ax over his shoulder and walked over to a tree stump]...I picked up my ax just like this and [with a mighty *whump* on the stump] cut it off just like that!"

Then came the well-practiced punch line. "So, boys, if a rattler ever bites you on the pecker, that's just what you gotta do."

Well, eyes bulged and jaws dropped, but by the time the boys had made the trip home, they'd convinced themselves that the whole thumb and ax yarn was just part of the day's entertainment. But not so, or at least not *entirely* so. Witnesses would write later that Trapper had sliced his thumb open, sucked out the venom and went on with his talk. But after several minutes he became wobbly on his feet and his alarmed guests rushed him to a hospital, where it took him six days to recover. Just who cut off the thumb tip isn't clear.

By 1940 the intrigue of Trapper Nelson's Zoo and Jungle Garden had begun to expand well beyond the town of Jupiter to a cosmopolitan cultural center just a mile or so away.

Just why takes some explaining. The southern tip of Jupiter Island, a 15-mile-long, half-mile-wide barrier reef, begins just across the Intracoastal Waterway from Jupiter. Whereas the average Jupiter family lived from fishing, farming or selling supplies, Jupiter Island was a private club, organized as a separate town, drawing bluebloods from around the world who had shunned garish, glitzy Palm Beach (15 miles to the south) by building a low-key, environmentally respectful, community of human-sized "cottages."

Chief among them was Joseph Reed, founder of the Jupiter Island Club and a man who probably did more than anyone else to enhance the fame and fortune of Vince Nelson. His first such impact was on Trapper's zoo. Explains son Nathaniel P. Reed, now perhaps Florida's foremost conservationist[7] and patron saint of the venerable Jupiter Island Club: "Back in 1940 I was seven years old. We had five guest rooms and I can hardly remember a time when they weren't full. Today we think in terms of having visitors for the weekend, but then friends from up north would come down and stay two, three weeks at a time. And all this meant having sure and steady ways to entertain them. Many were entertainers themselves — actors, producers, singers — because my dad backed a lot of Broadway productions.

"As part of making sure they had a good time, Dad had a 30-foot boat named *The Laurel* that he kept docked at Shuey's Fish Camp on the lower river. It seemed like at least every other week he'd take a party of eight or ten people out on that boat. And for me these times were magical. We'd start out by fishing for sea trout in the lower, wide part of the river, then we'd go in the middle part and troll for jacks and snook. When we'd get just beyond Kitching Creek, Dad had a spot that you couldn't see from the water, but where he'd cleared some of the jungle foliage and put in a grill and some picnic tables. At that point we'd haul out some gangplanks and go ashore to grill steaks or fish for a picnic lunch. Then just thirty minutes away would be the highlight of the trip, Trapper's Zoo and Jungle Garden.

"There he'd be in his shorts and pith helmet, usually with a couple of black snakes draped around him. And he'd have a way of just letting one slither onto the arm of one of the wide-eyed girls. I can still remember people buying baby alligators in little boxes made out of palmetto leaves. I shudder now to think that we might have had something to do with those stories you'd read from time to time about full-grown alligators being found in places like Central Park."

In the same sort of way, Trapper Nelson's fame spread well beyond the Loxahatchee. Because Reed entertained guests from Katharine Hepburn to famous Broadway producers — and because other Jupiter Islanders like Edsel Ford and heavyweight champ Gene Tunney all cruised upriver with *their* own entourages of houseguests — Trapper made for fascinating conversation at dinner parties from New York to London to Paris. Adds Nathaniel Reed: "It may be hard for some people today to envision, but back then, to all these northerners, the Loxahatchee was just as exciting as going up the Amazon. You expected to see Tarzan just around the corner — only in this case, there he was!"

The Jupiter Island connection helped both Trapper and the river. One time, just before the war, Trapper paid Joseph

Reed a visit with some disquieting news. The Tidewater Lumber Company had just gotten a contract to chop down and haul off every cypress tree they could lay their saws on. The graceful giants were often 300 to 400 years old, and suddenly the Loxahatchee was about to be raped and choked like a Maine logging stream. All Trapper knew was that Reed had two things he didn't — money and connections. Was there anything he could do?

A few days later Reed paid a call on the superintendent of the Tidewater Lumber Company. For show and friendly persuasion, he was accompanied by Gene Tunney, the one-time demolisher of Jack Dempsey and every lumberman's hero. After some signed autographs and man-to-man conversation with Reed and the Champ, the foreman agreed to accept a "personal contribution" from Reed in exchange for a promise to leave intact all the cypress standing along the Loxahatchee shoreline. In time, saltwater intrusion would take its toll on most of them, but the fact that some still stand is tribute to the love Vince Nelson and Joseph Reed shared for the river.

Meanwhile, Trapper Nelson's Zoo and Jungle Garden spelled economic opportunity for the same local teenagers who were selling fish for two cents a pound to help their parents stay afloat. Louis Freeman found an albino possum, which Trapper readily bought. Whenever Glynn Mayo could catch a rattlesnake, Trapper would buy it for $1 a foot. Ellis Roebuck specialized in turtles at 25 cents each. Of course the main attraction was just having the excuse to go to Trapper's. "He'd give us the run of the place," said Mayo. "The rope swing alone was worth the trip," added Roebuck.

Trapper usually found the most exotic snakes on his own treks across the jungle terrain upriver. One such trip illustrates the fact that not all of his visitors were welcome — even in those early years. The wilderness also attracted people who had good reasons not to be seen in public. Britt Lanier had some citrus groves west of Jupiter and recalled the time when a sheriff's deputy appeared at Trapper's compound to ask if he'd seen two men and a woman camping in the woods. He said they were wanted for questioning. What he *didn't* volunteer was that the trio was part of a gang wanted for bank robbery. Also left unsaid was that the bank had offered a $5,000 bounty — a sum the police officers wanted to carve up themselves.

The next morning, having forgotten the visit, Trapper strode out along the riverbank looking for snakes, an empty snake sack over his shoulder and a .38 pistol on his hip. He had crossed a couple of small streams when suddenly a man in uniform jumped out excitedly from behind the bushes and shouted, "Hands up! Hands up!" As the man trained a shotgun on Trapper, two bloodhounds burst out of the woods and pinned him beside a large tree. There they squared off for a long minute, with the nervous man shrieking, "Keep your hands up!" every few seconds.

Trapper's trail had paralleled a rough road, and Britt Lanier's truck just happened to be bouncing by on the way to one of his groves when he heard the commotion and stopped. "I'm a sheriff's deputy," screeched the excited gun wielder. "That man is a bank robber. I deputize you to go over there and take that sack from him."

Lanier started laughing — perhaps at the thought of what the guard would probably find if he reached in the sack. "When I told him who he'd caught," said the farmer, "the man was downcast indeed, having lost his chance at $5,000."

Sometime around 1938 the legend of Trapper Nelson took a brief detour to the fight ring. Very brief. As already noted, Joseph Reed and ex-boxer Gene Tunney were fellow Jupiter Islanders. One of their neighbors was Charles Francis Coe, a lawyer whose real love was promoting boxing matches and writing fight stories for the *Saturday Evening Post*. It seems that one Sunday Coe was part of a trip upstream that Tunney organized. As Trapper greeted Tunney and began some playful banter, they began to attract a crowd of curious gawkers. Seizing a theatric moment, the ex-champ playfully held his hand up to Nelson's. "Holy cow, mine looks like a lady's compared to his," Tunney said in mock amazement.

By the time the Tunney party was halfway back downstream, "Socker" Coe, as everyone called him, was bubbling about a new idea. Boxing was all the rage among young men from Jupiter to West Palm Beach and each Tuesday, a good boxer could count on a purse of $50 to $100 at the American Legion Hall on the north side of Clematis Street. Enlarged in 1930, the arena held up to 2,000 people, and on most Tuesday nights it was filled with the smell of sweat and cigar smoke and boisterous bettors from Palm Beachers in rep ties to farmers in straw hats.

Before long Socker Coe had worked out a heavyweight fight between the "Wild Man of the Loxahatchee" and a gnarly old pug from Texas named Tiger Long. Never mind that the only time Trapper had ever donned boxing gloves was when he'd first arrived in Jupiter and spent a few nights hanging around with other youths at the makeshift ring on the second floor of the schoolhouse. This seemed to matter not to promoter Coe. Before long the *Palm Beach Post*

sports writers were being plied with drinks and rhap-
sodized about a new contender who was "half Man Moun-
tain and half Mister America." No, he hadn't much of a
fight record because he was too busy wrestling alligators
in the jungle. But the writers could be sure he was training seriously for his debut by running barefoot to West
Palm Beach each day.

Actually, most of Trapper's training consisted of punching
a flour sack full of sand that he'd hung near his cabin.

More than a few lads from Jupiter piled into their fathers'
jalopies and headed for West Palm on the big night. Socker
Coe had whipped up a good crowd and added to the ex-
citement by having persuaded Trapper to enter the ring with
his hair matted in a crazed explosion that befitted "the Wild
Man of the Loxahatchee."

At the opening bell an unperturbed Tiger Long surveyed
his perfectly sculpted adversary and began circling him
slowly.

Beau Mayo was one of the Jupiter teenagers who boxed
over the schoolhouse, and he was among the local faithful
who'd followed their hero to West Palm for the fight of the
century. "What I remember most is that this other fighter
was a lot smaller than Trapper," says Mayo. "He feinted once
with his left hand, and when Trapper dropped his glove, the
guy popped him right on the button."

And that was it. Trapper toppled over like a jack pine.

"I guess he just must'a had a glass jaw," was Mr. Long's
only recorded comment.

Trapper never mentioned the episode again and no one
was brave enough to try rubbing his nose in it.

Lawyer-fight promoter Charles Coe would "manage" Nelson in another capacity that same year. It seems that Trap-

per didn't get along much with the man who owned twenty
acres to the east of his main camp. One H. J. "Hardy" Miller
became increasingly irritated when cars and hikers would
use the rough road that crossed his property on their way to
see Trapper. Besides, some of his goats had gotten themselves
caught in Trapper's snares.

One day Trapper drove to the post office and went next
door to Jupiter Sundries for some ice cream. Miller must
have followed him all the way, because he burst in right afterwards and tried to start a fight. "He cursed Trapper and
pulled at his arm and was very disagreeable," reported Bessie
DuBois much later. "The man [Miller] was small, with white
hair, and Trapper knew that if he knocked him down he'd
be jailed right away, so he took his ice cream and left."

Louis Freeman says it wasn't quite that way. "You had to
understand Hardy Miller," he says. "He walked around in
bib overalls and always had a chip on his shoulder about his
size. He'd fight anybody at the drop of a hat." He baited Trapper too long, says Freeman, and Trapper flattened him.

Bessie's *History of the Loxahatchee River* tells the rest:

> *Trapper had looked up the county records of the
> road to his place and it went back, he said, about
> one hundred years. Occasionally he had tried to
> improve the road. Trapper's antagonist first built
> a barrier of logs across the road, which the Trap-
> per and a friend [probably Joe Farrell] disas-
> sembled and threw into the river. Then the man
> built a barbed wire fence, which they also re-
> moved. Next they found a great pile of palmetto
> roots in the road.*
>
> *Eventually Trapper came home one day furi-*

> *ous. The county bridge had been set on fire. The*
> *county refused to fix it, so the Trapper and his*
> *friend repaired it as best they could. The Trap-*
> *per was so enraged the friend had a difficult time*
> *restraining him.*[8]

Well, Hardy Miller was getting on Trapper's nerves and his goats were getting into Trapper's gardens. One night a tremendous *BOOM* shook the woods. It was so loud it shook the bedposts in Louis Freeman's house six miles away in Jupiter. Hardy Miller raced toward the noise and found that his goat house had been blown to bits. Impaled all over the surrounding palmetto bushes were parts and pieces of 16 goats.

By noon the next day the still-apoplectic Miller was leading a team of armed sheriff's deputies over the crime scene. Trapper was arrested "on suspicion" of using dynamite illegally and tossed in the Martin County jail.

As locals chose sides and prepared to show up for what promised to be a first-rate court brawl, sheriff's investigators combed through Trapper's compound looking for evidence that he'd bought and used dynamite. None could be found, however. Nor were there any witnesses. So, for want of any clear evidence, the jury found Vince Nelson not guilty of the charges.

Nelson's attorney was the only one he knew — his fight mentor "Socker" Coe.

"How much are you going to bill me for this," Trapper asked him.

"How much you got?"

"I've got one hundred and ten bucks," said Trapper, probably fudging a bit.

"Then that'll be the fee," said Coe, who probably knew a thing or two about fudging.

The busy zoo, however, soon replenished Trapper's available cash, and it was not long afterward that he became an avid buyer of land along the Loxahatchee. At the time, undeveloped dry land could be acquired for less than $10 an acre. Swampland (most of which would be deemed valuable wetlands today) went for $2 and $3. But even that was too steep for most folks. Fran Hilsted Webb, who said her father "lost a fortune in the bust," added, "landowners had to pay taxes if they wanted to keep their property, and there was no one who could afford to buy any except at tax sales." For example, a landowner who owed real estate taxes for 1932 had five years to pay up. Lists of delinquents were published, and any citizen could schedule a hearing before a county judge and claim that land for a fraction of its value by paying the amount in arrears. If he paid taxes on time for the next three years he received the deed.

In the late thirties more people were selling or forfeiting land than buying. One reason was that in 1932 the federal government had paid bonuses of $500 each to World War I veterans. Some in the Jupiter area had used their newfound largesse to buy small plots, and after a few rough years of undercapitalized subsistence farming, many were throwing in the towel.

Even the area's mainstay, the asparagus fern business, fell on hard times. "The problem was that the asparagus fern tended to lose its needles rapidly," recalled one grower.

"Florists had begun buying wild huckleberry cut in the Cascade Mountains and we started losing ground."

Pelts and picnics brought cash to Trapper Nelson, and he began perusing the delinquent tax rolls to see what he could afford with his sacks of coins and clumps of crumpled bills. At first he seemed to have no particular area in mind. He bought bits and pieces in spots ranging from land around his upriver camp all the way down to shoreline on the Loxahatchee's North Fork.

Just how did he get the means to buy the more than 800 acres surrounding his camp? No official records exist to explain it. The most plausible story is a simple comment by Louis Freeman, who often accompanied Trapper in setting his lines. "He told me that Judge Chillingworth gave it to him," says Freeman, who now lives in Fort Pierce.

The relationship between Trapper Nelson and Judge Curtis E. Chillingworth — the same man who sentenced brother Charlie to life — is as mysterious as it is intriguing. Harvard-educated Chillingworth loved the Loxahatchee and become one of Trapper's closest fishing buddies in the thirties. Chillingworth was an avid buyer of tax-delinquent land and often competed directly with his fishing friend. Chillingworth was also at the center of a Saturday night poker game that always took place at — where else? — the main cabin in Trapper Nelson's Zoo and Jungle Garden.

Louis Freeman, who helped Trapper with his lines by day, got paid by night to keep the lanterns lit and fetch anything the players needed. "Oh, there'd be ten or twelve men there, sometimes with two games going at once," he says. "It was pretty much the courthouse crowd — the judges and lawyers who ran things in Palm Beach and Martin counties. Judge Chillingworth was always in the middle of it. There'd be a bottle beside each man, and I remember one of them laying a .40 pistol on the table just as a joke."

Trapper, who loved poker almost as much as snaring wild-cats, never played in these games, says Freeman. He made his money by being the "house" and collecting sizeable tips from grateful winners.

Yet, even the tips he got by day from Palm Beachers and the tips he got by night hosting poker games wouldn't explain how he was able to amass over 800 acres of prime Loxahatchee River frontage. Judge Chillingworth could no doubt answer the question, but he was murdered most gruesomely in 1954.[9]

Teenaged trapper in the Arizona desert with a wildcat,
soon to become a pelt. 1926? (PHILIP CELMER III COLLECTION)

Charlie Nelson, showing off before his latest "harvest" from trapping along Old Jupiter Beach Road, 1931. The car is no doubt the same one he drove to the police station after shooting John Dykas. (PHILIP CELMER III COLLECTION.)

Trapper Nelson in front of his first cabin – the first of dozens of photos with snakes as a backdrop. Probably 1933. Note the attempt to emulate Tarzan attire. (FLORIDA HISTORY CENTER & MUSEUM ARCHIVES.)

Trapper's camp as seen from the water, probably 1938.
(JONATHAN DICKINSON STATE PARK ARCHIVES AND PHILIP CELMER III)

Trapper chats with boat
captain Dave Brooker
during one of his regular
tourist visits, probably 1938.
(DAVID AND AGNES BROOKER)

Trapper at around age 30, with
young day-tripper, name unknown.
(FLORIDA HISTORY CENTER & MUSEUM ARCHIVES)

In this 1938 photo, Trapper is standing atop the metal roof of his boathouse, looking down on his camp.
(JONATHAN DICKINSON STATE PARK AND PHILIP CELMER III)

A typical day's catch for Trapper on the Loxahatchee, 1938.
(PHILIP CELMER III COLLECTION.)

Part of Vince Nelson's immediate family, taken during a summer vacation trip to Trenton, New Jersey in 1940. From left, standing: Vince, his father Casmier, and sisters Marcie, Connie and Nell (wearing Trapper's pith helmet). The males, identified only as Pete, Mike, Ed, Kenny and Dave, are never mentioned in his correspondence, or as ever accompanying his sisters when they visited on the Loxahatchee.

(PHILIP CELMER III COLLECTION)

Wartime:
Reluctant Soldier, Happy Scout
1941 – 45

The 1941 *Farmers Almanac* listed the population of Jupiter, Florida at 311. After Pearl Harbor it would be considerably less for a few years as young men raced to recruiting stations to join the war effort. Recalls Roy Rood: "Don Lainhart Sr. was in charge of the draft board. He told me that out of 145 men between the ages of 17 and 38, only three were found physically unfit for the draft."

For those left behind, life changed markedly, starting with the impact of both ocean and river. Natural erosion had almost closed the Inlet at the time and the u.s. Coast Guard quickly finished the job in 1942 by filling the slender opening with sand from jetty to jetty. For the next four years the Coast Guard maintained stables on Juno Beach. Each day its men patrolled the narrow key by horseback or with dogs as they searched for u-boat activity and survivors of sunken Allied ships.

It was a severe blow to the fisher folk of Jupiter, but war was war and they had to make do. To avoid silhouetting Allied ships, the lighthouse removed its 250-watt bulbs and replaced them with a single 60-watt household light. Dodie Dubois

Hawthorn remembers complete blackouts at night. "If we used our car after dark we had to shade our headlights so they couldn't be seen from the ocean. Blackouts were partly the reason Mother had to close the restaurant during the war, but gasoline rationing and the lack of some food products also had to do with it."

The precautions weren't farfetched at all. U-boats patrolled the coast off Jupiter Inlet. Margie Freeman remembers hearing three torpedo explosions in one night and Raymond Swanson six on another. "We'd feel the bed lurch slightly, then look out the window to see the flames of a torpedoed ship," recalled Swanson. Eventually the Coast Guard patrol came upon a one-armed man living in a tent near Old Jupiter Beach Road. He spoke English like a native and called himself a hobo, but one night a stakeout caught him beaming signals to the U-boats at sea. He'd been a German saboteur all along.

An explosion of a different kind took place in the population three miles to the north of town. Soon after the war began, the military requisitioned or leased 11,364 acres along the northwest side of U.S. Route 1 for the Southern Signal Corps School. It was known better as Camp Murphy (for a pioneer in the development of radio beams) and became *the* nation's center for research and training in the emerging science of radar detection. When it became fully operational in July 1942, $5.3 million had been spent on living quarters, cafeterias, a theater, complete utilities plant and classrooms for 854 officers and 5,752 enlisted men.

For the most part, the heart of Camp Murphy was well north of the Inlet and thus away from "downtown" Jupiter (pop. now 250 or so). But Camp Murphy acreage sprawled all along the upper Loxahatchee — including Kitching Creek, where

Trapper and the DuBois family both had owned some plots that they'd used for holiday outings. Says John Dubois III: "All I know is that the government told Trapper and my grandparents that it needed their land and that they'd get it back when the war was over."

Neither party ever reported getting a dime for their property, but what it might have fetched at the time was indicated by a letter a neighboring Kitching Creek landowner wrote John DuBois in April 1942. One C.D.S. Clarkson, who had since moved to Virginia, told his neighbor that he'd received a letter from the War Department offering to pay $240 for his 120 acres along Kitching Creek. Clarkson asked DuBois if he'd received a similar letter, then offered an opinion: "I replied that the price was confiscatory and that I would not accept less than $5 per acre for the high land and $3 per acre for the swamp of 10 acres next to you."

Such were land prices in 1942.

At first, World War II scarcely affected Vince Nelson, nee Natulkiewicz, in his lush jungle preserve. Pearl Harbor came a month after his 33rd birthday, and by now he was more bronzed and thickly muscled than any movie Tarzan. At Trapper's Zoo and Jungle Garden the fruit trees were prospering, the cages were full of interesting animals and now a guesthouse had been built for family visitors and occasional paying guests. Word about Trapper had spread to Palm Beach, and people whose names identified Fortune 500 companies began gliding their Criss Crafts up the Loxahatchee to get a look at a legend in the making.

For a growing number of ladies, watching Trapper's muscles ripple was probably a greater attraction than gazing on pens of alligators and snakes. Carroll Little (now Dorsey) was just 17 at the time and would hear the women buzz around her as Trapper gave his lectures. Dorsey visited the camp often because her father, Richard Little, and Trapper were great friends. She'd stay overnight in the guest cabin as the men went spearfishing in the moonlight.

Trapper still retained that awkward distance towards women that Bessie DuBois had observed early on. Says Carroll Dorsey: "I remember one gal who worked in the solicitor's office down in West Palm Beach. She thought he was some catch, and one day she talked herself into the boat with Trapper, my dad and me when we went down to Jupiter. She was quite lovey-dovey to Trapper all day, and when we were making our way back that evening in the boat, she insisted that the two of them get off and walk the rest of the way on a path that led back to his camp. When they finally strolled back to the cabin I couldn't help asking her how things went. 'Oh, he's just a good Boy Scout,' she said with a laugh."

But later in 1942 Trapper got himself snared by a more determined woman. Her name was Lucille Gee and she worked at her mother's bar, the Nineteenth Hole on u.s. Route 1 down in Lake Park. Richard Little and his daughter Carroll accompanied the two on May 6 when they went to the Justice of the Peace in West Palm. "I remember that my dad had to lend him a sport coat and tie for the occasion," she says. "He looked *so* uncomfortable standing there in front of the j.p. Afterwards he threw off the tie and we all went to the Nineteenth Hole and had a cracked conch dinner.

"Lucille was tall, with very pretty coal black hair and lovely skin," recalls Dorsey, now a widow living in California. "She was a bit heavy set, but very voluptuous. Dad and I liked her, but a lot of Trapper's friends didn't. They thought she was after his money."

Indeed, locals were already gossiping that Trapper had made a lot of money and, having scant use for it, simply stashed it around his camp. But in this case, the yen to marry may have had more to do with the fact that Vince Nelson thought it would exempt him from the draft.

Actually, in the summer and fall of 1942 Trapper was often seen at Camp Murphy, but not in army garb. His Jupiter Island friend Joseph Reed had enlisted as a captain and had somehow managed to get himself assigned to the new radar training base just across the Intracoastal from his beloved Jupiter Island. There, Reed was made responsible for building camp morale. Despite the nebulous job description, he took his mission seriously. Reed used his own money to hire a ferryboat to shuttle soldiers to Jupiter Island for R&R and again to build a beachfront pavilion where local ladies would serve snacks and help the many under-schooled youngsters write letters home.

Reed also oversaw the three huge mess halls at Camp Murphy that served round-the-clock meals. Problem was that all too many men were being bitten by rattlesnakes on their way to mess and/or stung by deadly black widow spiders lurking around inside. The solution: hiring Trapper Nelson to be in charge of "Predator Removal." Recalls Nathaniel Reed: "My dad paid Trapper $50 a week out of his own pocket, and he took the job seriously. He collected hundreds of black widow spiders and put them on display at his zoo."

Eventually, not even a new wife or Captain Reed's special needs could save Vince Nelson from the draft. In late 1942 he got his letter from the War Department and soon found himself dispatched to a basic training camp in Texas. Sometime

soon afterward, Private Nelson tore a thigh muscle doing cal-
isthenics — an injury that would produce a hasty operation,
a permanent crater in his leg, a slight limp and a transfer to,
of all places, Camp Murphy. "It was like the story of Br'er
Rabbit and the Briar Patch," his friends in Jupiter would say.

Just how it happened — and what Trapper Nelson came
home to — is shrouded in rumor and conflicting memories.
One hears of "society people" pulling strings, although Nat
Reed, for one, professes no such knowledge. Then there's
the story about an affair involving the daughter of a cabinet
official in Washington.

As for Lucille, the newlyweds had agreed that she'd look
after the camp and feed the animals until her husband returned. However, "she just wasn't the backwoods type you'd
need to oversee a jungle camp," says Carroll Dorsey. Yet,
many locals insist that Lucille did find it commodious enough
for entertaining various gentlemen from nearby Camp Murphy. When Nelson arrived back in Jupiter he was told that
Lucille had run off with an Army colonel and was working
as a waitress somewhere near Port St. Lucie. He never saw
her again (but would, as we shall see, become well acquainted
with her attorneys).[10]

Trapper began his career at Camp Murphy as an MP, pa-
trolling the perimeter and pulling guard duty at the front
gate. But making Vince Nelson wear a regulation uniform
was like putting a business suit on one of his alligators. Private Nelson received a reprimand once for cutting his military trousers into shorts. He also racked up AWOL charges
for repeatedly disappearing in a U.S. Army jeep while he
tended to his zoo. He had also used his unprecedented, four-
wheeled freedom to drive over to Vleck's Oceanside Service Station on U.S. Route 1 and hang out with guys like

Beau Mayo. "I thought he always looked like Humpty Dumpty when he drove in all hunched over in that little jeep," laughs Mayo.

During many wartime weeks, Trapper's Zoo and Jungle Garden had more guests from Camp Murphy than from the civilian population. He'd cook for his army friends, but would never tell them exactly what was on the menu. "Some kind of animal," he'd answer the squeamish. "You can eat anything you want if you know how to cook it." After dinner they'd get down to poker, craps and other serious business. One might call it trapping by moonlight except that the objective was another kind of "game."

Eventually, the brass at Camp Murphy decided to make an accommodation with the pied piper who was leading so many men off base. Someone recalled that Trapper (before being drafted) had once led a rescue party to a navy plane that had gone down in the Loxahatchee wilds. So a new job description was drawn up that called for an MP "scout" who would patrol the base perimeter looking for spies and such. And yes, he could have a jeep for use on the job. Since the camp borders touched on Trapper's own land, no one could complain too loudly if a considerable part of his duty time took him in that vicinity. Although the war kept Nelson from trapping as much as he'd like, he wound up skinning his poker playing soldier guests for $1,500 — most of which went to buy more land.

IV Celebrity Hermit

1945 – 60

War's end unleashed a wave of free time, money for recreational spending and gasoline for motorboats — all of which began to wash upriver to Trapper Nelson's Zoo and Jungle Garden. And the host was ready for it. The camp now boasted of two rough but serviceable guest cabins, a 100-foot-long covered boathouse, a diving board, three rental rowboats and a metal-roofed chickee hut enclosing long rough-hewn tables for picnics. Off to one side was a pistol range where visitors could sharpen their shooting at Trapper's homemade targets.

Just above in the chickee hut was a loft where Boy Scout and other youth groups would often spend a night telling ghost stories, then trying to sleep amidst strange new sounds. "I was one of those kids," recalls Eric Bailey, who now runs Canoe Outfitters of Florida a few miles upriver from Trapper's camp. "The way he'd make sure no one would run around the camp at night was to have us all climb up to the loft on this crude wooden ladder. Then he'd take the ladder away until the next morning. All I remember is that we didn't sleep much because the mosquitoes ate us alive."

Supporting the expanded complex were a hand-pumped

well, water tower and labyrinth of irrigation pipes. A three-bay garage housed Trapper's army-surplus jeep and a sawmill, powered by a 7 H.P. Briggs & Stratton motor, that was used mainly for making shipping cages for animals. Nearby, he'd dug a ditch and built a platform over it so he could change the oil in his jeep.

Everything seemed to have a reason and a multiple use. The bamboo shoots, for example. The shorter thin ones were cut down for fishing poles. Medium-thick shoots might be used for poling a boat over the shallows while the largest - which grew to sixty feet - could be harvested for roofing the chickee hut. Even the pistol range had another use. Trapper would collect the lead from spent shells and melt it down for irrigation pipe castings.

He still trapped, but now it was within more disciplined constraints. Most mornings he'd arise and religiously chop a cord of firewood. Before long the woodpile became so high and long that one observer likened it to a "freight train without wheels." Trapper used a double-bladed ax and swung so furiously that onlookers had to stand yards away to keep from being hit by flying chips. His hands were so large that he broke several axes until he finally had them custom-made with especially thick handles.

After breakfast he'd check and re-set whatever traps he'd laid out in the woods that week. Gators were now a protected species. Years of winnowing had put in a dent in the population, and now Trapper needed the survivors to loll about on the riverbank so that approaching tourists could say they'd been to a real jungle.

Around 10 A.M. the first visitor boats would begin appearing around the bend. Others would arrive in his newly cleared parking lot. Most would head first to one of the two out-houses just behind the docks. Their second stop invariably would be the pens and cages of animals. As a visiting *Palm Beach Post* reporter described it:

> *Packed tourist boats plied the Loxahatchee, bear-ing city folk...who were treated to the exotic sights of caged bobcats, raccoons, several species of tur-tles and still more alligators, all captured by the Trapper himself within a few miles of the zoo. The real sensation was a six-foot concrete snake pit brimming with deadly rattlesnakes — a hor-rific sight etched in the mind of many a tender-foot.*
>
> *Other cages were devoted to less dramatic species of snakes: poisonous water moccasins, harmless black snakes and indigos which the Trapper would occasionally drape around his neck for the benefit of awe-struck guests.* [11]

When those guests were little children, his presence was awe-some indeed. Several years after Trapper died, Gerry Knam of Hobe Sound wrote the *Jupiter Courier* of his first visit as a grade-schooler.

> *At the [entrance] we saw Florida panthers and other wild animals in wire cages. Behold, there stood Trapper Nelson, who was a BIG man! As the line approached him to pay him a quarter, the girl behind me said "They say he killed his wife up here!"*
>
> *Scared was not the word for it when I had to put what seemed to be a very tiny quarter into*

*his rather LARGE hand. I was just glad to get
away from him.*[12]

But Elizabeth Roebuck Wood, now of Beverly Hills, Florida,
has a much different impression:

> *I lived on Loxahatchee River Road, a few miles
> from Trapper Nelson's camp. To get a few cents
> in our pockets for the things our parents had for-
> bidden us to use, such as cigarettes, some of us
> collected gopher turtles for Trapper. He paid us
> 25 cents each for them.*
>
> *If he had ever liked kids to begin with, we might
> have cured him of it. Trailing our bicycles
> through the ruts of the hot, sugary sand of his
> truck lane was usually a pack of hound dogs.
> They turned his camp into an orchestra pit of
> snarls, growls and hisses.*
>
> *But he would smile as he took the croaker sack
> squirming with gophers, patiently count the
> money into our sweaty palms and go off some-
> where with them. When he was out of sight we
> would take the liberty of using his stout rope swing
> to fly like Tarzan over the river for a refreshing
> splash into the cool water full of alligators.*
>
> *But we never saw a gun in his hand, and he
> never spoke a harsh word. Tolerant and kind —
> that's the other side of the "wild man of the Lox-
> ahatchee."*[13]

To adults, Trapper was clearly "outdoor chic," as a *Post* reporter put it, and his showmanship was part of the reason

why. He'd pop up at a family picnic in the chickee hut and suddenly drape an eight-foot indigo snake around the neck of a petrified girl. Some people deliberately brought extra food because they knew he'd come and mooch some — which also meant they'd be the center of attention for a while. And just to keep all eyes on *him*, some say the Trapper would occasionally cut off the head of a gopher tortoise, drink its blood, and give his startled audience a lecture on the virtues of wildlife nutrition.

Although audiences would invariably remember the indigo snake first (several actually starred in the role over the years), Trapper's most long-lived pets were his dog Bozo (a rat ter- rier with a strong strain of mutt) and Stumpy. The latter was a ten-foot alligator who would have been longer had it not been for the fact that rival males over the years had bitten a foot or so off his tail and most of one leg. Stumpy's special status was reflected by the fact that he had his own cage and rated special billing on the lecture tour. Once when Stumpy got loose during a big storm, Trapper spent the better part of several mornings searching for him on the riverbanks until he was found at last and restored as star attraction.

The languid trip upriver, the animals, the starkly different way of living and the articulate, entertaining host brought people from all walks of life, and the fare (adults 50 cents, children a quarter) was well worth a day's outing. Besides Gene Tunney and Edsel Ford from Jupiter Island, Palm Beach delivered such notables as 1940 G O P presidential can- didate Wendell Wilkie, Gary Cooper and Patricia Neal (hid- ing from the gossip columnists during a famous love affair) and various Whitneys, DuPonts and Kennedys. Locals would jabber about high-living Palm Beach ladies whose idea of chic was to slip away for a weekend in the jungle and play

Jane to Tarzan of the Loxahatchee. According to one breathless account in the *Palm Beach Post*, a "striking young woman" — a direct descendant of President James Monroe — was smitten as soon as she reached his dock on a boat from Palm Beach.

> *As the Trapper, naked to the waist, went through his act of wrestling alligators and flirting with snakes, the young lady's mind turned forever from pale diplomats. Throughout the rest of her family's Florida winter she would disappear for days at a time and return home with brambles in her stockings and a smile on her face.*[14]

How much of it was true and how much legend by imaginative locals? "It doesn't square with the man I knew," says a close friend. "But I can't say it isn't true because he was a man of so many dimensions."

Brian Sheedy, a friend from Palm Beach who often fished with Trapper, found him a colorful raconteur — in and out of the wild. "On the river he always knew just the right spots to fish and always had an endless supply of amusing anecdotes about woods life," said Sheedy. "He came to dinner at our house as well and he was not at all the uncouth 'wild man' he was supposed to be. He did eat enormous amounts of food, like the time he consumed two full loaves of bread before attacking the entrée. He always kept us interested as he told of his land deals and stories about amusing camp incidents. I liked him and so did my family."

Trapper's Polish-Russian roots were never evident to friends and visitors. Nearly everyone thought he was a Swede, as the name Nelson seemed to confirm. However, his real roots were exposed one day when a group of Polish American club members arrived in a "boat-a-cade." As Trapper greeted them at the dock, he heard some of them wondering aloud in Polish if they could make a small fire to heat their lunch. Without a word, Trapper built a fire for them. When their cook called out in Polish that the sausages and cabbage rolls were ready, Trapper showed up at the table with the rest. As he consumed half the group's picnic, he admitted that while he couldn't speak their language, he could understand it. But he said nothing about his ancestry.

Local teenagers loved hanging around all that action at Trapper's Zoo and Jungle Garden. When Elton Phillips was growing up, he'd drive his father's tractor up to the camp on Sundays. "There were always tourists who were stuck in the sand and would pay us to tow them out," he recalled. "We'd spend every weekend at Trappers. He was real nice. If he liked you, he'd do anything for you. And he was good to young people. He bought all the snakes we could catch and bring to him. Why he'd even pay a quarter for a dinky-donk stupid snake. He shipped them off to zoos all over the country."

Fact is, Trapper was playing all the angles in the fifties. He sold animals to zoos and wholesalers. He sold hides of otter, bobcat and rattlesnake to Sears Roebuck. He sold mail-order orchids and air plants, and kept racks of each at dockside for boat trippers to buy for their patios. The camp also sold post cards imprinted with "Trapper Nelson's Zoo and Jungle Garden." He grew sugar cane and snapped off pieces for sale to his visitors. He rented rowboats and poles for fishing. You could buy baby alligators and raccoons direct from Trapper's cages and firewood from his never-ending woodpile. He even sold artifacts made from the heads of gators, garfish and snakes, which he soaked in a vat of formaldehyde behind his private cabin.

Vince Nelson loved people, but on his own terms. An average day might produce around thirty visitors. He would take pride in escorting them about, even baiting hooks for children and telling them where to dig for worms. But come mid-afternoon when the tourists returned to their cars and boats, the camp once again became his first love — a place of solitude.

Another generally unknown dimension of Trapper is that even then he was not always alone. Friends would take turns visiting, cooking for and caring for the man who always seemed to be at the center of their attention.

During the summers, Carroll Dorsey, her two brothers and her father Richard Little would come often. "My parents were divorced and we kids mostly lived up north with our mother," she says. "But summers we'd come down to be with Dad, and much of the time it meant staying in one of Trapper's cabins. Dad was a photographer in Palm Beach, and you wouldn't think he'd have much in common with a trapper. But the two were a lot alike. My dad was big like Trapper and he'd spent a lot of time in his youth hoboing."

And they both loved spearfishing — almost always by moonlight after Carol and her brothers had gone to bed. Trapper and Little would take the battery out of the jeep and lug it into a rowboat. Then Trapper would hook it by wires to a miner's light he'd affixed on his pith helmet, thus providing a beam that would shine into the water and bring curious fish to the top. Illegal, of course, but who was to stop Vince Nelson at midnight in his Loxahatchee hideaway?

"There in the moonlight they'd spent hours just talking about the old days and philosophizing about everything," says Dorsey. "My dad read a lot and so did Trapper. They could talk on just about any subject."

Here's another surprise. Vince Nelson never lost contact with his sisters and their families in Trenton. During his earliest years on the Loxahatchee, he often returned during the muggy summers to visit his father and sisters, and when he was first homesteading upriver they would send him packages of clothes, cookies and bed linens that he couldn't get in Depression-ravished Jupiter.

After the war Trapper soon had regular visits at the zoo from his sisters Marceline (Marcie), Nell, Emily and Connie and their families. For the next twenty years or so the most frequent summer visitors among them were his oldest sister Marcie Celmer, her husband Phil Sr., their grown children and grandchildren. Every summer Trapper would drive his army-surplus jeep up to the Stuart train station and meet the Celmers, who would spend their entire two or three week vacation living in another world from their native New Jersey.

Phil Celmer Sr., a machinist at a large gas turbine factory, quickly became one of Trapper's closest friends. "Vince was good with lumber but never all that handy at things like plumbing and electrical engineering," says Phil's daughter-in-law Lucille. "It was my husband [Phil Celmer Jr.] and father-in-law who helped him add new improvements such as the sawmill, the water tower and a hand-cranked drill press."

Trapper's sister Marcie and her daughter-in-law Lucille were just as valuable. They'd take charge of the kitchen and try to see that Trapper had more variety in his diet than possum, raccoon and gopher tortoise. "Vince had two ways of cooking," says Lucille, in her late seventies as this was written. "One was to boil whatever it was with barley and gruel. The other way would be pan-fried with flour or fried dough. I remember one time when he went to town and brought back a sack of flour that was full of weevils. When I complained about it he said, 'Don't worry about it. It's all good protein.'

"One day when I made some comment about needing more variety on the table," continues Lucille, "Vince walked down by the river to the rattlesnake pit and grabbed one by the neck. And that's what we had for dinner. Of course I should add that he was also careful to skin it and pin up the hide. Then he'd take the jaw out because it would be soaked in formaldehyde to remove the skin, then put on the stand he had down by the river and sold to some eager tourist."

After dinner, with no sounds outside but frogs croaking and mullet splashing in the river, Trapper would get out the cards and badger the Celmers into playing poker, canasta or whatever small stakes contest he could dredge up from his hobo and army days. "I was no card shark," remembers Lucille, "but he'd keep me there 'til all hours. He especially loved blackjack. No matter what cards he was dealt, even if it might have totaled 17, he'd always have to go for 21. One time when he was losing and out of money, he disappeared behind the cabin and came back with some crumpled bills with dirt falling off them. When I asked where he got them, he just said 'You'll never guess.' Another time he told me, 'Oh, I've got money hidden all over my pineapple patch.'"

Perhaps no one remembers those summer visits more

vividly than Phil Celmer III, now a retired air force colonel. "My parents first brought me down to Trapper's in 1949," he says. "I was four years old. Not long afterwards he gave me a bolo knife and started calling me 'Little Trapper.' He'd take me on morning walks and let me set trap lines. Sometimes in the afternoon we'd pile into his jeep and drive down to the Pantry Pride grocery where he'd buy me a pint of ice cream. Can you imagine anything more glorious for a kid than having your own bolo knife and all the ice cream you can eat?"

By the time young Phil was twelve (the family called him "Flip") his proudest moment had been catching a dangerous coral snake and selling it for $6 in cold cash. When he was 13 Flip had a dream come true when he got on a train without his parents to spend the first of two entire summers as his great uncle's aide de camp.

"It was hard work but the most fun I've ever had," says Celmer, who now lives in Waretown, New Jersey. "He gave me my own .22 long rifle and I went with him everywhere. We'd start in the early morning with just hot tea and maybe some donuts. First we'd go out and check the trap lines. Then it would be hosing down the animal cages and irrigating the fruit trees and garden with an elaborate system of pipes my grandfather and Dad had linked to a pump house."

After that the chores would be varied but never-ending. "To help feed the caged animals, my job was to set rat and mouse traps all over the place," says Celmer. "Mostly they went to feed the snakes. The gators liked mullet and just about anything else. I remember once we had a gator that hadn't eaten in what seemed like months and months. One day I caught a turtle while fishing. He had swallowed the hook, so I knew he was going to die. When I came back from the dock with the turtle hanging from my fish line, I stopped at the alligator cage and saw this old gator lift up his head. When I dangled the turtle in front of him, the gator just crunched the shell and ate the turtle, hook, shell and all. That was the end of his hunger strike."

On some afternoons Trapper and his protégé would use the tanning table at one end of the main cabin to stretch hides over boards. On another day they might be outside the cabin washing down and skinning dead animals, or cooking cypress knees in a big 55-gallon drum so they could strip off the bark and sell them as souvenirs.

Also in back of Trapper's cabin (and out of sight to tourists) were a few cages with animals that were wounded or in need of special attention. If they required surgery, Trapper was his own amateur veterinarian with a supply of ether for anesthesia. And because the zoo kept skunks and sold some for pets, Trapper would first perform surgery to remove the scent glands. "Sometimes it worked, sometimes it didn't," says Celmer.

Late afternoons were times to do something special. Often Flip and Trapper would just lie in their hammocks in the chickee hut after a day's work, looking down the river, and drinking a can of Coke from the old propane refrigerator that stood nearby. "Sometimes we'd take the jeep down to Jupiter Island. There we'd load up with driftwood and coconuts, which we'd sell to tourists at the dock. Or we might pick up a load of shells, which Uncle Vince thought were good as nutrients for his mango trees. One time he had gotten a letter from my parents saying it would be nice to have a sandbox for the younger children when they next visited. So Uncle Vince's idea of creating a sandy beach was to load a whole truck full of sand and haul it out to his riverbank.

"We used to ride the jeep through the waves at the ocean. He could do that because he'd taken the trouble to have copper brake linings installed. One day we were charging through the surf and wound up coming back home with a giant sea turtle strapped to the back of the jeep like a spare tire."

They might also drive to town for ice cream or visit Captain Frank, the tour boat operator, in his ramshackle house on the Intracoastal. The inside, to young Flip's endless fascination, was crammed with driftwood, knickknacks and curios gleaned from a lifetime of beachcombing.

"Uncle Vince and Frank enjoyed ribbing each other," recalls Celmer. "Trapper would always poke fun about the time when Captain Frank and a friend decided they'd bring up an abandoned undersea cable and strip off the rubber insulation so they could sell the copper. Well, I guess they didn't know what to do with the big pile of rubber that was left when they were finished, so they decided to burn it. When they put a match to it, they set off a plume of black smoke that could be seen all up and down the Florida coast.

"I think the hardest thing I ever got involved in at that point in my life was when Uncle Vince paid Captain Frank $35 for an abandoned seventy-foot yacht," says Celmer. "His idea was to bring this old wooden thing up to the camp and use it at the dock for picnics. It had no engine, so the two of us used thick bamboo poles to walk that big old boat ten miles up the river. When we finally got back to the dock that night we were both so tired and thirsty that it was the first time I ever saw Uncle Vince pop open a beer."

Celmer, now with his own growing boys, remembers his great uncle as a quiet and gentle man. "He had a way about him that made you want to work hard just in hopes of a compliment. He seldom raised his voice, but you knew if you screwed up you didn't do it again. I recall one time, for example, when we were hunting in the woods and I was carrying my gun barrel up high. 'Fool! Don't ever do that again,' he said. And I never did. Or there was the time when the land crabs were migrating. Another boy and I got our BB guns and used a bunch of crabs for target practice, then just left them in a pile. After a while the stench around camp got so bad that Vince finally figured out the cause of it. He said 'Don't you *ever* kill an animal unless you have a useful reason.' And I never did again.

"To this day I cannot fail to remember him as a great man to learn from and be with," says Celmer. "He paid me 50 cents for every rat or turtle I caught, and in six weeks he set up a bank account for me and we put $35 in it. We sat in his jeep in the August heat and ate a quart of chocolate ice cream each. I was 13 and life was beautiful. I loved him."

V   *Alone Again*

1960 – 68

On August 3, 1960, Vince Nelson wrote a one-page letter to his sister Marcie. "I caught a coon this morning and the cruise had 14 people," he said amidst routine chitchat. On September 8 he wrote her husband Phil Celmer Sr. After grumbling about two weeks of steady rain, he announced: "Have closed my camp to all the public including the cruise. Now I feel a lot safer, as it was a real risk in many ways dealing with the public."

Indeed, he quickly gated the dirt road entrance to Trapper Nelson's Zoo and Jungle Garden. Down came the rope swing and parts of the dock. The big picnic boat disappeared. Pines and cypress were toppled so that they fell across the river and blocked all incoming boats. Signs were posted on trees and on the riverfront:

**NO TRESPASSING
PRIVATE PROPERTY
NO BOATS BEYOND THIS POINT**

Nailed to a tree beside the pineapple patch was another sign that read:

DANGER — LAND MINES

Suddenly, locals began changing their perceptions of Vince Nelson — from eccentric to dangerous, from recluse to paranoiac, from stoic to stormy.

And everyone in town had their own theories as to why. "I know he worried about the plans to extend I-95 and the Florida Turnpike up our way," said his friend John DuBois. Indeed, all around this island of wilderness, he could feel the rising tide of Florida development. A million people now stretched along the hundred-mile-long coastal corridor from Miami to Fort Lauderdale to Boca Raton to West Palm Beach. Jupiter-Tequesta, at its northern tip, was still seen as rural by the urbanites who pressed against it from the south, but the fish camps and family grocers had already given way to oceanfront condos and gated golf communities. And anyone who drove eight miles west of the ocean on Indiantown Road would find the former wilderness dotted with citrus groves, cattle farms and "equestrian" developments featuring homes on five and ten acre plots.

Trapper also worried about visitors that he couldn't handle alone. He was now past fifty with a waistline to match his massive chest. Prosperity and population growth meant more people hiking and boating to the camp — increasingly the wrong kind of people. Gangs of teenage boys would foul his traps or sneak up at night and taunt the Legend of the Loxahatchee in some sort of Rite of Manhood. Soon, Trapper found himself even varying the days and times that he went to town for staples just to throw off vandals and robbers.

"I think a lot of the trouble had to do with him deciding to rent out his guest cabins to strangers," said DuBois. "They attracted a pretty rough crowd." Adds grandnephew Phil Celmer: "Each of the gator cages had a wooden top on it, and it seemed that every time somebody got drunk he'd want to walk on top of them and try to rile up the gators. I remember one time a guy lifted the top and actually fell in. I think the gators were more scared then he was."

All of the above underscore another reason for closing the camp: fear of lawsuits. Trapper luckily had escaped litigation in the fifties when a boy had been injured on the rope swing and when another kid was run over by a motorboat just off his dock. By 1960 Vince Nelson's steady attention to the delinquent tax rolls had netted him nearly 1,100 acres, or more than three miles of prime land along the increasingly desirable Loxahatchee. And he feared that he could lose it all in one liability case.

How acute were these fears? Phil Celmer III remembers that during part of his first summer with Trapper, a "very good-looking lady [whose name he can't recall] was living at the camp along with her son, who was about my age. I know it was pretty serious between them because at one point Uncle Vince wrote her into his will. But two or three years later her son ran over someone in a powerboat down in Lake Worth. Vince was so worried that he might be held partly liable if they married that this more than anything caused the relationship to fall apart."

His fears were also fueled by government regulators. The first such visit to Trapper Nelson's Zoo and Jungle Garden resulted in its exasperated owner being compelled to obtain a $10,000 security bond for keeping poisonous snakes on his property. Soon afterward he was required to start paying state sales tax on his visitor fees.

In 1959 or '60 the health inspectors followed. "The out-houses are unsanitary," they declared. So Trapper installed concrete bathrooms with running water. When the job was done, the new facilities were judged unsatisfactory for entirely different reasons (the same ones are approved by and used by the state park today).

Next came environmental inspectors. "You don't have a system for eliminating animal waste from your cages," they said.

"Sure I do," answered Trapper. "I hose them out every day or so." "Yes, but that means creating a runoff that will find its way into the river and increase water pollution levels."

"Well, what do you think the animals were doing when they lived in the woods?"

It was all too much. Maybe he really was tired of the public. With young Flip Celmer now in college with his own busy life, with the elder Celmers available only for a week or so in the summers, maybe the whole thing was just too much for one tired man.

All of the above are true in part. But Vince Nelson had endured threats of teenagers and lawsuits before. The real reasons he closed the camp in August 1960 were worries over land, money and family — in precisely that order.

The land-money-family tale begins and ends with a dilemma. While Trapper Nelson loved his vocation and cherished his solitude, Vince Nelson — numbers whiz and shrewd businessman — couldn't wait for throngs to migrate into Martin County and push up the value of his land. His letters to family in New Jersey are full of hopeful rumors that "a big aerospace outfit [namely Pratt & Whitney] is going to build a rocket plant near Indiantown" or that "RCA is looking at land to build a plant in North Palm Beach." He clipped building lot prices out of the local papers and sent them to his brother-in-law Phil Celmer Sr.

One reason for reporting all this encouraging news was that Trapper had a slight hustler streak himself. In 1951 after buying over a hundred acres of raw land near the North Fork of the river in Tequesta, he convinced his brother-in-law to buy an adjoining 45 acres for $3,000. At the time there was talk of building a bridge over the North Fork that would link to U.S. Route 1 and bring an onrush of eager homebuyers. Phil's plot would fetch a whopping price with a few acres left over to build his own retirement haven.

By 1960 Vince Nelson found himself like a lot of so-called land barons — rich and poor at the same time. On the plus side of his ledger, land values were rising indeed. On the debit side, annual real estate taxes were ballooning proportionately. He wrote Phil Sr. that his county tax bill had risen 350% in one year and that his expenses including lawyers "will run over $10,000." All the hides and air plants and 50-cent admission fees had never added up to more than $3,000 a year. Now, instead of preying on tax delinquents, he was about to become fair game himself.

Added to the debit side was the fact that Phil's heart was failing and his wife ailing. They looked to an early retirement and were counting on selling their 45 acres for much of the nest egg.

What to do? First, Trapper went to the savings and loan where he had a small account and tried to borrow the money. But of course the S&L didn't want some log cabins and cages as collateral, and the applicant had no immediate prospects of a big all-cash land sale to repay a long- term loan.

In September 1960 Trapper finally managed to wrangle a five-year, $100,000 loan at a steep 10% yearly interest from

George Offutt, a Hobe Sound businessman who chiseled a nice niche for himself by lending to people who dwelled outside the comfort zone of banks. But being able to bring his tax bill up to date didn't allow Vince Nelson to breathe easier once he got home and read the fine print in his loan contract. It had no amortization, instead requiring interest payments on the full $100,000 every six months. It also gave Offutt the right to seize all of Trapper's nearly 1,100 acres should he miss a single mortgage payment or a tax deadline. Thus, the man who never made more than $3,000 a year would now have to pay $10,000 a year in interest *plus* new property taxes on 1,100 acres whose book value was rising every year.

Interestingly, days after he banked the rest of the $100,000 loan, Trapper bought the senior Celmers' 45 acres for $10,000 down and a mortgage for $90,000 (or roughly $2,500 an acre) to be paid over five years.

Why would a supposedly shrewd land dealer shackle himself like that? First, he clearly thought he was rescuing his best friend from anguish and helping him to retire. Second, he figured that the remaining $75,000 or so from the first loan would be enough to live on, pay Offutt his 10% interest, pay the Celmer mortgage and meet the real estate taxes on the rest of his properties before the five-year note came due. But well before that doomsday deadline he'd sell a big chunk of his own land into a rising market, pay everything off and still have a pile to live on for life.

But reality decides not to follow the script. Months go by with no takers. Yes, the state is still planning a bridge over the North Fork, but work hasn't started yet. Legal fees for just keeping his ownership intact run way over estimates. To keep out snoopers and squatters, Trapper decides to ring his entire four miles of upper Loxahatchee property with fence post and barbed wire — another heavy cost. Taxes keep ballooning. He's forced to request that the senior Celmers forego principal payments on their note and let him pay just interest. But Phil is ill and anxious for cash. He goes in for a pacemaker implant. Within a few weeks it "backfires" and is removed. Trapper writes Phil Sr. bluntly that "you haven't much time left" and pleads for the Celmers to come to Florida and rent an apartment near the new medical center. They talk of it, but by March 1963 Phil is dead at 65. By year-end sister Marcie is gone, too.

By early 1964 Trapper is barely able to make his semi-annual interest payment to Offutt. Offutt hovers overhead like a turkey buzzard, waiting for a tax infraction or legal judgment to swoop down and feast on all of Trapper's property and bank accounts.

But now comes a ray of hope! John MacArthur, the biggest Florida land baron of them all, has recently acquired 4,000 acres next to Trapper's "and now wants to reach the river so he can build a town of 100,000." If he makes a reasonable offer, Trapper will sell the ranch.

MacArthur's people play the mating game. But after all that parrying, all they want to do is offer Trapper some stock in one of their companies. He's insulted. They must think he's a dumb bumpkin. MacArthur's a thief just like all the big developers and their lawyers.

By now Trapper is corresponding with 42-year-old Phil Jr., Flip's father and the heir to his parents' modest estate. But now the chemistry's not quite the same. Phil Sr. was Trapper's best friend. His son is family, to be sure, but they didn't quite confide in each other like equals — more like uncle and nephew, mentor and youth.

Besides, Phil Jr. is a world-class worrier. His own small business in New Jersey is in serious trouble — all while he's trying to raise four kids and send Flip to college at an extra cost of $2,500 a year. He's desperate to cash out those 45 acres Trapper bought from his dad on time payments. But instead Trapper sends a letter bomb. It announces that he can't even pay the interest due, let alone buy the land for cash. In fact, he warns that if Phil doesn't find a way to loan him some cash towards his next interest payment on the Offutt loan, it's all over for both of them. He sternly reminds his nephew that the note for the 45 acres is subordinate to Offutt's $100,000. "Fail on that and we've failed on everything."

By now family relations are like a high-tension wire strung from Trenton to Jupiter.

More anguished months go by. Trapper puts up LAND FOR SALE signs around the North Fork and advertises in the *Stuart News*. No takers. But another ray of hope brightens the horizon. Work is definitely starting on a tall span across the North Fork, and developers are sniffing all over the place.

By summer 1964, the August 24 deadline on the five-year Offutt loan is fast approaching and Trapper is more than $11,000 behind in his interest payments. Now the man who always closed his letters with "wishing you luck" finally gets some. Bessemer Properties, with pockets almost as deep as MacArthur's, approaches him with talk of paying in the $1,500-per-acre range for 200-plus acres, including the Celmer spread. It's hardly the $4,000 per acre he's been telling his nephew the land could be worth, but it's better than having one's carcass picked by vultures.

A deal is struck. Smiles and handshakes all around.

Now the lawyers begin due diligence. Question: is there anyone who might have a lien or other claim on the land? A former wife, for example?

No, says Trapper. The only wife he ever had was properly divorced years ago.

What jurisdiction granted the divorce?

St. Lucie County.

A fastidious Bessemer lawyer drives to Port St. Lucie and looks at the court records. He tries to find a Lucille Gee living in the county but can't. Back in Jupiter, he asks some folks the same question and they all say, "Lucille? Oh, sure. She moved back to the area several years ago. She still works down at the Nineteenth Hole in Lake Park."

In early August Trapper and Bessemer are visited by lawyers for "Mrs. Lucille Nelson." Their claim: In 1945 Trapper's war bride had not settled down in St. Lucie or in her native Lockport, New York, so she never could have read the public notices issued by the estranged husband. Fact was, she'd never been properly divorced, and now she wants her wifely "dower" or share of whatever money Trapper gets from the land sale.

Vince Nelson is stupefied. Then he's steaming. He's had it with thieving developers, conniving lawyers, and now, scheming ex-wives. He's ready to walk away from everything. The hell with it. He'll go somewhere else and start out trapping just like it was 1931 all over again.

Phil Celmer Jr. can hear the bellowing all the way up in New Jersey. Writing on a yellow legal pad, with a sheet of carbon paper to preserve a copy of his letter for posterity, he pours out all of his tensions and frustrations. "I was surprised that you would deliberately break the contract with Besse-

mer without having another offer in hand," he writes. "It
looks like financial suicide to me."

Now it's the nephew lecturing the immature uncle:

> *With the foreclosure it looks like you leave the*
> *North Fork, have deficiency judgments pending,*
> *interest payments outstanding, be unable to pay*
> *your taxes, and still have the ex[wife] to contend*
> *with and interfere with future land sales.*
>
> *I believe that cleaning up the divorce would be*
> *your prime target rather than fighting Bessemer.*
> *You could not lose all your property on her ac-*
> *count because community property cannot ex-*
> *ceed 50% and [unintelligible].*
>
> *You say that all big operators are legal crooks.*
> *I don't believe little people could handle a deal*
> *of such magnitude. Sooner or later you have to*
> *deal with the big operator. I also don't believe a*
> *big or reliable outfit would deal with quit claim*
> *deeds, which give no guarantees or warrantees.*
> *They can't afford to be uncertain.*

Phil Jr. chides Vince for excoriating the Bessemer lawyer who
sleuthed out his backwoods divorce tactics. Instead, he says,
the attorney is no more than "an expert well-paid to thor-
oughly investigate the facts for his client." Then:

> *The whole business gives me a sinking feeling in*
> *the pit of my stomach. I can understand how you*
> *feel because I am going through the same sort of*
> *thing here. My business is just hanging on. We*
> *lost over $20,000 last year and came within three*

days of going bankrupt last month. We have an
agreement with the bank that when our net quick
assets drop below what we have in the bank we
are to go bankrupt voluntarily. This month
started out bad and keeps us in a constant sweat.
I have the job of trying to hold off creditors. For
10 days I've been waiting for the deal in Florida
to go through so I could say to hell with this rat
race and start fresh in Fla.

When I scraped up the $500 I loaned you re-
cently, I said it was the best I could do at the time,
and things are even rougher now. I borrowed
money from the insurance policy at 6% interest.
[Here he lists other debts pressing in on him.]
My back will not stand an additional strain at
this time. I am in no position to speculate or lend
money.

I thought you had a last chance with Bessemer.
Without an alternative offer I don't believe you
need worry about losing everything to the ex-wife.
It looks like foreclosure, deficiency judgments,
taxes, lawyers and judges won't leave anything
for anyone. Allowing this foreclosure doesn't make
sense to me at all.

I wish you luck, and you sure need it. - Phil.

It's now 1:30 P.M. on August 24. Judgment Day — literally.
Lender Offutt is inside the Martin County Courthouse waiting for the clock to strike two so he can officially foreclose
on 1,100 acres of prime Loxahatchee property and scoop up
any cash found in Vince Nelson's bank accounts.

Outside on the courthouse steps, all eyes are on the large

man with his familiar pith helmet and khaki shirt. He listens
with a studious frown as two Bessemer lawyers explain the
terms of their last offer. The "εx" has agreed to waive her
dower rights for $30,000 cash and two waterfront lots worth
around $5,000 each. Trapper won't have to face her. Instead,
Bessemer will handle the matter and deduct her payments
from the land sale price. Their final offer for 214.9 acres of
land will be $322,350 — all cash — or around $1,500 an acre.
Offutt will be paid off from the proceeds.

Phil's letter seems to have sunk in. At 1:45, fifteen minutes
before the guillotine will fall, Vince Nelson signs.

To the local media and friends in Jupiter, the Legend of the
Loxahatchee had cashed in big time. They didn't know about
or tally up the chunks taken by Offutt or lawyers or taxes.
Nor did they grasp that other landowners around the North
Fork were already selling for $2,500-$3,000 an acre. All they
knew was what they read in the papers. Trapper Nelson, that
crafty old recluse, had held up some guys in suits for $322,350
in cash. He was rich! And no doubt he was already busy bury-
ing his treasure all around the rangy riverfront property he
still owned!

In truth, it was actually April 1965 before all the post-sale
lawyering was completed and money exchanged hands. By
that time, Bessemer was well into planning what would become the Riverbend and Turtle Creek country clubs on its
new land. Trapper, after paying Offutt $114,000, the Celmers
their $90,000 (plus interest in arrears), "wife" Lucille her
$40,000 blood money, and a slew of legal and tax bills, fig-
ured that he netted around $63,000. He complained that

compared to what he'd paid for the land in taxes over the years, he actually lost on the deal. But for the first time his remaining 857 acres were free of tax and mortgage debt.

With more money in the bank than he'd ever had before, Trapper was encouraged to "upgrade" his lifestyle. He bought a few modern appliances (still powered by propane — never electric) and was soon eating store-bought steaks from a new freezer.

After 1964, Nelson continued to trap off and on. His letters to Trenton continued to reflect the same youthful zest for the hunt, boasting in one of them about a morning that netted two wildcats even though a lifetime of mornings had produced similar trophies. But consistent results were getting harder to come by. One reason Trapper had been able to sell all the raccoon skins he could trap was that they'd be made into coonskin caps for kids who were caught up in the Davy Crockett rage. Now, as the TV show's ratings waned, so did the price for coonskins.

But trapping wasn't the only thing changing. Outsiders claimed to see a dour, slower moving, husk of a man, and his actions often seemed to confirm it. By then, if anyone wanted to see Vince Nelson about anything, they had to send him a post card and then wait for a reply by mail. Only a few friends had keys to the lock on his gate. His shotgun was always at his side. They say he once caught two men hunting on his property. At gunpoint he took away their two rifles, broke them over a stump and told them he'd kill them if he ever saw them again.

Sometime in 1967, Dick Little drove up to Trapper's locked

gate, got out of his car, and started to walk the remaining half-mile to visit his old spearfishing friend. Little had gone only a few yards when he saw Trapper step out from behind a tree in the distance, cradling a shotgun. "What do you want?" the voice called.

"Trapper, it's me...your old friend Dick."

The man by the tree raised his gun. "I don't have any friends," he shouted. "Go away now or I'll start shooting."

By 1968 Vince Nelson was often sick and consistently in discomfort. John and Bessie DuBois would insist that it had all begun with a change in eating habits. The two restaurateurs, who had been observing the legendary appetite longer than anyone else, said that once Trapper sold the 215 acres to Bessemer and bought his freezer and refrigerator, he began eating "fancy steaks and other foods that didn't agree with him.

"He was always complaining about gas," added John DuBois. "Said he thought he had colon cancer. But when I'd try to get him into a clinic he'd refuse. He'd always have some reason for mistrusting doctors and hospitals. One of them I remember was that his brother-in-law had gone in to have a heart pacemaker inserted and died a short time afterwards." He had also seen his old friend Captain Frank, a pipe smoker, wither away from cancer of the throat.

One reason why the DuBois family still saw more of Trapper than anyone else is that he'd drive into town to use their outdoor pay phone. At the time, John and Bessie were among a very few friends and relatives who knew that Trapper was working on a deal to sell all of his remaining 857 acres to the new Jonathan Dickinson State Park while also obtaining rights to remain on the 100 acres around his cabin until he died.

The "deal" had begun a few months before when Charlie Smith, a land acquisition agent for the state Division of Recreation and Parks, thought he'd pay the area's largest landowner a friendly call. Unaware of the reception that men like Dick Little were getting, Smith had parked by Trapper's gate and walked most of the way to the main cabin when a large man with a shotgun stepped out of the doorway.

Without waiting for a "Who goes there?" Smith pointed over to the large woodpile and said with a big smile, "Show me the man who could cut a pile of wood that big!"

Trapper leaned the gun on the cabin wall, flexed his muscles and said, "*I* cut that pile." Within a few minutes Smith was sitting in a chair inside the cabin explaining what a wonderful addition a pioneer trapper's place would make to the park.

Again, Trapper wrote his family in New Jersey that "if the price is reasonable," he'd sell, even though he thought state agencies just as crooked as developers. And as if to take out an insurance policy of sorts, he contributed $1,000 to the campaign of Republican governor Claude Kirk.

The terms must have been right, because before long Trapper had at least two lawyers negotiating the fine points, and the DuBoises would get a blow by blow account as he bellowed instructions over their outdoor pay phone.

By July 1968 Trapper had another problem as well. He was urinating through a catheter. "He was convinced he had prostate cancer," says Carlin White, who saw Nelson on a Friday after he'd been in town to buy supplies. "Dr. John Prince, one of the finest physicians in the area, had told him he didn't have cancer, but he had this idea in his head and wouldn't let go of it. Yet he wouldn't go to the doctor, either."

It may have been on the same day in late July (probably the 26th) that Trapper pulled into Joe Vleck's Oceanview Service Station on U.S. Route 1 to leave his jeep for some minor repairs. "He was in obvious pain," recalled Vleck. "He'd been eliminating through a tube for some time and admitted he hadn't seen his doctor in six months. So we ran him up to Dr. Prince's office. The doctor was pretty mad about his staying away for so long and he yelled at him for a while. Then he gave Trapper a prescription for some pills. We went with him to Jones Pharmacy where he had it filled before heading home."

Vleck drove the repaired jeep out to Trappers' the next day and left it at the gate. Trapper stepped out from behind a tree in the distance. The two exchanged waves. "And that's the last I saw of him," said Vleck.

On Tuesday, July 30, the weather was its usual 90 degrees, but uncommonly dry — a rarity for the subtropics in summer. The morning *Stuart News* reported that north-south traffic on the Florida Turnpike had risen 14.9% in the first quarter of the year, second highest of any major U.S. roadway. Realtor Ralph Hardman advertised a "3 br home on ½ acre w/100 ft. river frontage" for $18,000. A front-page headline read: FAST OUTBOARDS CUT CHANCES OF SLOW MANATEES. Another one exclaimed: SIX SQUARE MILES OF LAND SOLD WEST OF PALM CITY FOR $875,000. The Publix advertised chuck roast at 59 cents a pound and the Winn Dixie offered "4 cans of chunk tuna for $1." On the editorial page, columnists ground away at Vice President Hubert Humphrey for being too hawkish on Vietnam and Senator Gene McCarthy for pandering to peaceniks.

Henry "Tot" James and his wife Helen sat reading the *News* and rocking on the front porch of the DuBois fish camp, pausing often to look at their watches. James had been a friend and fellow trapper with Nelson in the thirties. He'd written Trapper on July 14 saying that the couple would be visiting South Florida for a couple of weeks and sure would love to see their old friend before returning to their Indiana home. Nelson had replied, saying he'd meet them that morning at the DuBois place.

After a couple of hours with no Trapper, the two simply had to get back on the road, so they left for Indiana. John DuBois thought it just wasn't like Vince Nelson to break a date like that. On a hunch, he called the post office and asked if Trapper had been by in the past week to pick up his mail.

No, he hadn't. At that point DuBois decided to drive out to Trapper's camp. After unlocking the chain gate (he was the last friend to be allowed a key), DuBois walked up a rough road now nearly impassable with overgrown weeds. As he approached the main cabin, the many guinea hens that roosted in the nearby trees stirred up a racket that pierced the quiet summer day. Inside the cabin everything seemed in order except for the lack of an occupant.

DuBois began walking about the camp, but soon found himself guided toward a strange smell. It quickly became almost unbearable, and as he approached the picnic chickee hut by the river, he knew why. There was Trapper's body, sprawled in the sand, face down. His 12-gauge shotgun lay on the sand a few feet away. One shell was discharged. The shell apparently had entered the chest and traveled upward through the back of the head.

DuBois knew immediately that any coroner would have a tortuous time documenting details. The body was badly decomposed. Guinea hens and raccoons had been picking at it for days in competition with swarms of maggots. What was left of the brain looked like mushroom soup.

Because of the body's condition and the unhappy prospect of bringing it into an enclosed facility, a county pathologist conducted an autopsy of sorts on a picnic table in the chickee hut. That night the body was taken to a funeral home in Hobe Sound and cremated.

On August 6, in a small ceremony in the same chickee hut where he died, Vince Nelson's ashes were cast into the Loxahatchee. Since the will, adhering to his life-long aversion, stipulated that "no religious services are to be performed at my funeral," his nephew's wife, Lucille Celmer, read the *Requiem* that Scotland's Robert Louis Stevenson wrote for his own epitaph:

> *Under the wide and starry sky*
> *Dig the grave and let me lie:*
> *Glad did I live and gladly die,*
> *And I laid me down with a will.*
> *This be the verse you 'grave for me:*
> *Here lies where he long'd to be;*
> *Home is the sailor, home from the sea,*
> *And the hunter home from the hill.* [15]

Strange, but when police investigators, friends and family
had departed, no one seems to have thought of the camp itself — the cabins, the rental boats, jeep, dozens of traps, the
freezer full of food, the stacks of old *Wall Street Journals*.
The consequences of this oversight would later be severe.

Luckily, Trapper's caged animals fared better. Seventeen-
year-old Sylvia Pennock was not only passionate about
wildlife, but also curious as to what happened to any animals
that might still be caged on Trapper's property after his death.
A few days after the body was found, she persuaded her
boyfriend to drive to the locked gate and walk with her to a
compound that now seemed frozen in time.

"I remember how eerily quiet everything was," she says. "I
recall turning the handle on the cabin door and walking right
in. There was a chicken in the refrigerator looking just like
it was supposed to be tonight's dinner."

Another door led to Trapper's bedroom. In all the days Phil
(Flip) Celmer had spent with his great uncle, he had always
respected this inner sanctum as off-limits. Sylvia Pennock did-
n't know any better. She turned the doorknob and walked
into a room that would have passed a sergeant's inspection
at Camp Murphy. Hung and neatly pressed beside the bed
were Trapper's old army uniforms. "I remembered thinking
that I might expect to see a stack of girlie magazines in a bach-
elor's bedroom," she says. "But no such thing. Everything
was neatly in its place and nothing at all had been disturbed."

Outside, the zoo cages were empty save for a couple of small
alligators. "The one exception was the gopher tortoise pen,"
she recalls. "When I let the tortoises out, they were so hungry that they ran over to the closest thing they could find —
an old brown branch — and started devouring it."

Trapper at 40:
still showing the Tarzan physique on the beach in Jupiter, 1948.
(PHILIP CELMER III COLLECTION)

Inside Trapper's guest cabin in the summer of 1949:
sister Marcie, Vince, grandnephew "Flip,"
sister Nell and Flip's mother, Lucille.
(JONATHAN DICKINSON STATE PARK AND PHILIP CELMER III)

Brother-in-law Philip Celmer III and son Phil Jr. try out the mechanical saw just installed in the garage they built for Trapper in 1948.
(JONATHAN DICKINSON STATE PARK AND PHILIP CELMER III)

Six-year-old Philip ("Flip") Celmer III helps himself in Trapper's orange grove, 1949.
(JONATHAN DICKINSON STATE PARK AND PHILIP CELMER III)

Lucille Celmer, daughter of Phil and Marcie Celmer, does dishes the old fashioned way outside her guest cabin at Trapper's camp, 1949.
(JONATHAN DICKINSON STATE PARK AND PHILIP CELMER III)

Thirteen-year-old" Flip" Celmer's summer with Trapper in 1956 included cleaning lots of fish like these as well as chores that ranged from setting traps for animals to setting traps for mice to feed the snakes.
(PHILIP CELMER III COLLECTION)

Trapper in his late thirties,
when he embodied
"outdoor chic"
to people in
Palm Beach,
Jupiter Island
and well beyond.
Note indentation
above his right knee,
caused by his
only war "wound,"
a botched operation
on a thigh muscle
injured during
basic training.
(FLORIDA HISTORY CENTER & MUSEUM)

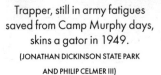

Trapper, still in army fatigues
saved from Camp Murphy days,
skins a gator in 1949.
(JONATHAN DICKINSON STATE PARK
AND PHILIP CELMER III)

Trapper in his fishing boat, with
unidentified boy in back.
Mid-1950s.
(FLORIDA HISTORY CENTER & MUSEUM)

Loxahatchee River Area

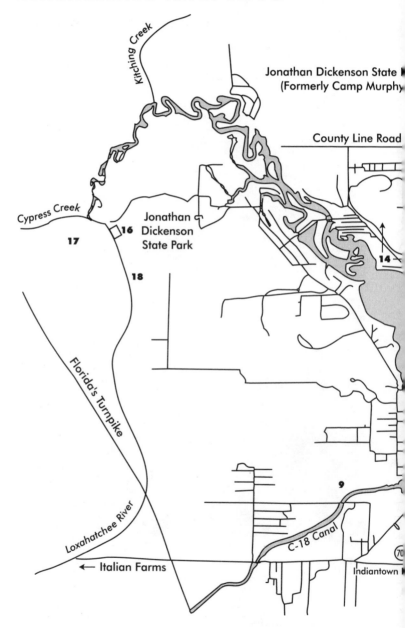

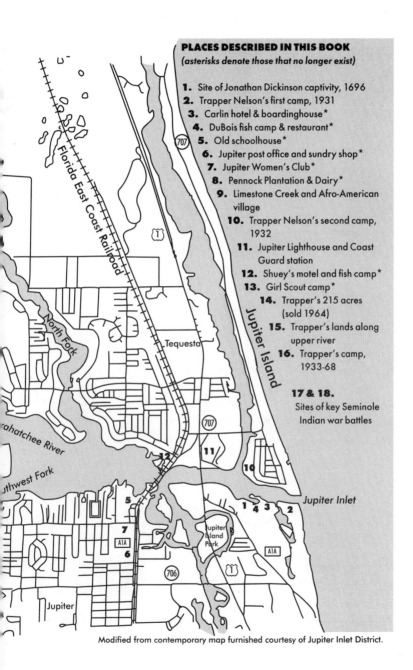

PLACES DESCRIBED IN THIS BOOK
(asterisks denote those that no longer exist)

1. Site of Jonathan Dickinson captivity, 1696
2. Trapper Nelson's first camp, 1931
3. Carlin hotel & boardinghouse*
4. DuBois fish camp & restaurant*
5. Old schoolhouse*
6. Jupiter post office and sundry shop*
7. Jupiter Women's Club*
8. Pennock Plantation & Dairy*
9. Limestone Creek and Afro-American village
10. Trapper Nelson's second camp, 1932
11. Jupiter Lighthouse and Coast Guard station
12. Shuey's motel and fish camp*
13. Girl Scout camp*
14. Trapper's 215 acres (sold 1964)
15. Trapper's lands along upper river
16. Trapper's camp, 1933-68

17 & 18.
Sites of key Seminole Indian war battles

Florida East Coast Railroad

North Fork

Tequesta

Jupiter Island

...ahatchee River

...thwest Fork

Jupiter Inlet

Jupiter Island Park

Jupiter

Modified from contemporary map furnished courtesy of Jupiter Inlet District.

Trapper's Camp Today

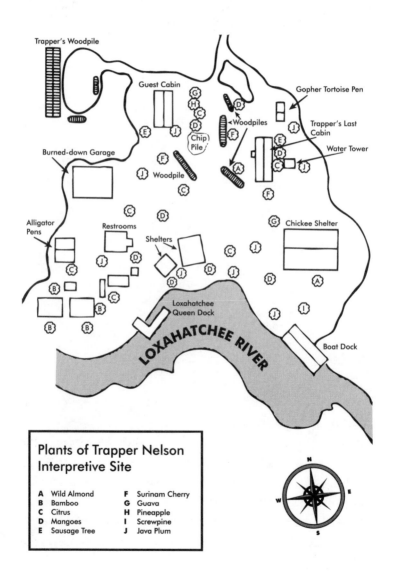

Trapper's Woodpile

Guest Cabin

Gopher Tortoise Pen

Woodpiles

Trapper's Last Cabin

Water Tower

Burned-down Garage

Chip Pile

Woodpile

Alligator Pens

Restrooms

Shelters

Chickee Shelter

Loxahatchee Queen Dock

LOXAHATCHEE RIVER

Boat Dock

Plants of Trapper Nelson Interpretive Site

A	Wild Almond	**F**	Surinam Cherry
B	Bamboo	**G**	Guava
C	Citrus	**H**	Pineapple
D	Mangoes	**I**	Screwpine
E	Sausage Tree	**J**	Java Plum

Who Shot Trapper Nelson? VI

On August 28, 1968, a six-member Martin County coroner's jury convened to determine officially the cause of Vincent Nelson's death at age 59. News reporters and several curious locals had shown up as well. As they waited for the proceeding to start, "we started swapping stories about Trapper," recalls one old-timer. "It was almost as if we were fishing on the river and talking about an old friend."

Then the county coroner, Harvey Piley, opened the inquest and sternly reminded everyone that they were there to investigate a grisly death — possibly a murder. Pathologist Dr. Leon Powell, who had led the on-site autopsy, estimated that the shooting had occurred about three days before discovery of the body. "It was obvious that there was a large gunshot wound in the left chest, approximately three inches below the nipple," he testified. "And the gunshot left a hole in the skin about one inch in diameter. It went straight in, through the lung and through the tip of the heart, which produced, undoubtedly, a rather rapid demise.

"As a matter of fact," said Dr. Powell, "the skull was so exposed that there was just a small amount of soft tissue on the back of it. It was fortunate for our examination that he was shot in the chest. If he were shot in the throat or through the arteries, we never would have found any evidence of it because all this was eaten away."

Slater Grose, who took part in the examination as a Martin County deputy sheriff, noted that the shotgun had shown no fingerprints because it had been covered so long by sand and tracked over by wildlife. Yet, he insisted that no evidence was found to place anyone else at the scene. "There was no indication in the loose sand of there ever having been anyone within a hundred foot circle around the [chickee hut]." Grose added that he'd walked the riverbank in search of any trace of someone tying up a boat or running one up on the shore. "There were no traces of anyone. There was no indication of any struggle anywhere and no foul play."

Deputy Grose called the wound clearly self-inflicted, adding that the investigation was "very extensive" and had produced a stack of paperwork "about 18 inches high.

"All indications were that he put the [shotgun] to his chest and pulled the trigger."

Several friends and acquaintances were sworn in. "Was Vincent Nelson the kind of man who would commit suicide?" Coroner Piley asked each one. Most of them equivocated. However, it was Pat Snow, a Tequesta savings and loan officer and executor of Trapper's will, who appeared to have the most impact on the jury. "He seemed obsessed with the idea that he had cancer," Snow later told a *Palm Beach Post* reporter. "Once when he was leaving my office he asked casually how my wife was, and when I told her she had died of cancer six months earlier, he sat right back down and pressed me for details. He was always concerned about being a burden on people, and he once confided to his sister that he'd rather die than be an invalid." [16]

Much later, Stuart police captain William Snyder re-read the evidence and applied it to his own experience. "You factor in all of these circumstances that were known at the time," Snyder said. "He [Nelson] thinks he's got cancer. He's becoming antisocial. You have names of people who testified that 'I'll kill myself before I'll become a burden.' You have no evidence of a murder. You have a guy lying there with a shotgun at his feet and gunpowder on his chest.

"Like in poker, you have to play the hand you're dealt. In any case, a detective looks at three components: witnesses, physical evidence and suspect testimony. In this case, I have no witnesses and no suspect testimony. All I've got is my physical scene. What does the scene say? The scene consists of a suicide."

"Might it have been an accident?" the coroner had asked.

"You don't accidentally shoot yourself in the chest with a shotgun," said Detective Snyder. "You accidentally shoot yourself with a handgun, maybe in the leg or in the hand. Theoretically, the guy could have been holding the shotgun saying 'I wonder what it would be like to kill myself someday'...and he mistakenly squeezes the trigger."

But in this instance, Snyder was reviewing the life of a man who owned and used guns all his life without any known mishaps.

After an hour or so of deliberation, the coroner's jury ruled the death a suicide. One irony, later volunteered by pathologist Powell, was that Trapper's body showed no signs of cancer. "I would have been able to see any cancer that had spread," he said.

Indeed, Dr. Prince, Nelson's own physician, had written

that the patient was told he didn't have cancer and that his stomach problems weren't serious. "He had been given all the reassurance that a physician could give him, but he believed not one word of it," concluded Dr. Powell.

And yet. And yet.

The jury verdict was supposed to put the Trapper Nelson matter to rest. In fact, it was but the switch that ignited a burst of theory and rumor from people all over Jupiter.

Most of Vince Nelson's personal acquaintants simply didn't buy the decision on a gut level. "I knew Trapper," lamented Grace Roselli, who so fondly remembers the kind and considerate man who welcomed her friends on high school Skip Day. "I can't for a minute believe he was the type of person who would do that to himself."

From Norman Brubaker, a ranger at Jonathan Dickinson State Park: "He was quite a guy. Suicide? Well, suicide has always seemed to me like a city man's disease. There's something about all these woods and water that just doesn't go with it. I don't think so."

P. A. (Bill) Lund, a conservationist who had been lobbying for the incorporation of Trapper's land into the state park, couldn't imagine it for two reasons. First, "he'd have to pull the trigger of that big shotgun with his toe to make it go off on his stomach," Lund would say often. "Then there's economics. He'd recently received over $300,000 from that land sale and was finally square with the world."

Indeed, Trapper was about to become a millionaire. Negotiations to sell the state all of his property at upwards of $1,500 an acre were just a smidgen away from fruition in July

1968. "It's kind of an American dream, isn't it?" mused one of the old-timers who sat in the gallery at the inquest. "So here he is, about to become a millionaire, and he goes and kills himself. Why?"

Louis Freeman, who spent as much time with Trapper as anyone, adds that "He would often tell me that just as soon as his land sale went through, he was going to travel the world and see all the sights he'd been reading about."

Beyond the matter of opinion, people began to ask why the official investigators hadn't delved deeper.

Item: Why was Trapper dressed in the clothes he wore when going to town? Why were the keys to the jeep lying on the picnic table beside him?

Item: Why would such an experienced handler of guns choose to kill himself in the clumsiest of ways? Why not train the barrel directly on his head rather than the chest?

Item: Police had removed the shotgun before it could be fully examined. The gun showed no fingerprints. Not even Trapper's. Moreover, the two shells in the double-barreled chamber were different. The shot that felled Trapper was a 12-gauge *Xtra-range* shell, presumably fired from the right chamber. Yet, still intact in the left one was a 12-gauge *Western Super X* rifle slug.

Item: The absence of footprints around the body would hardly be evidence of suicide, as investigators claimed. For Trapper to enter the chickee hut, *he* would have to produce footprints. No footprints at all would prompt suspicion that a killer could have taken a palmetto branch and wiped away *two* sets of footprints.

Finally, folks close to Trapper insisted that he kept his long guns and ammunition hidden in a rack behind the headboard of his bed. It was said that he feared state or federal regulators would try to confiscate his land or his right to bear arms on some technicality. If so, the shotgun would emerge only if someone were on the property to threaten him.

And from whence would come those threats? From many people whose paths he'd crossed, said the many who advanced conspiracy theories. There were those who would kill just to get at the treasure he supposedly had buried about the place. Some of these might even be the same teenage toughs who were known to show up to threaten an ailing, increasingly defenseless recluse. Said Bill Lund: "After he closed the [zoo], he told me that one of the basic reasons was because of his trouble with, as he called them, 'teenage hoodlums,' who would come out to challenge him to a fight or something, because in a gang they felt they could beat Trapper. On two different occasions he told me that he was very concerned about this because he didn't want to hurt anybody...."

Then there were those old scores that might have been settled. Trappers he'd chased off his property. Maybe someone was hired by big developers who saw him as a nuisance blocking their plans for river access. Perhaps it was the neighboring landowner who had built a wooden dam on a creek in the fifties, only to see it blown apart by Trapper (who even carried off the heavy boards the neighbor had used to build it).

Another theory: Trapper had harbored fugitives in the woods from time to time and eventually he just "knew too much." People whispered stories (although never documented) that Chicago mobster Al Capone regularly hid out with friends in Italian Farms (today's Jupiter Farms) just west of Trapper's land and near the family homestead that spawned actor Bert Reynolds. Locals told tales of digging up bodies on the "Capone" property, meaning that Trapper just might have stumbled on something during one of his hunting treks that he shouldn't have witnessed.[17]

But always the official investigators were ready to drag out the record and replay it for the critics. Example: the same guinea hens that shrieked when John DuBois came on the property were Trapper Nelson's early warning alarm against intruders. Anyone who sneaked up upon him would do so at his own peril.

But that's exactly what happened, some old-timers insist. Ruby Fortner Lanier, who still talks in machine-gun bursts at age 91, states that Trapper and her husband Elzie were good friends, and that Nelson told him often that Charlie was coming back for him. "In fact, he told a lot of people: 'My brother said to me I'm going to jail, but when I get out I'm coming to kill you.' And he would always end it by adding, 'And he *will*, you know.'"

Lanier and some others insist that Charlie had been seen in the area the week before Trapper was shot. Had Charlie the lifer been paroled? Thanks to a helpful state official who delved into a musty file folder in the "inactive records" room of the Department of Corrections, a fax arrived just before this book went to press. Charles Nelson, prisoner #23701, had been released on November 20, 1951.

Charlie had plenty of time in which to carry out his 36-year-old threat. What puzzles Richard J. Procyk, who headed the homicide division for the city of Miami Beach before retiring to Jupiter, is that the Nelson death apparently was ruled a suicide and the case closed without anyone trying to locate Charlie Nelson. Says Procyk: "You just don't close an investigation without interviewing the number one suspect or at least trying to contact him and learning where he was at the time."

Whether the authorities could have found Charlie remains questionable, given that not even his family knew his whereabouts. In any case, Trapper's surviving relatives just don't buy the revenge theory. "The idea that Charlie would have done him in is probably a one in a thousand chance," says Lucille Celmer. "We saw him once after he'd gotten out of jail [she can't recall just when]. He was at least seven years older than Vince and by then an old man who had been beaten in prison."

Lucille's intuition tells her something else. "Vince always said he'd blow his brains out if he ever became an invalid. By 1968 he was sick and he was also unhappy with the way society was going," she says. "Whether it was colon cancer or prostate problems or something else, his gut was bothering him acutely. I just think that in a moment of anger at the whole thing he just trained his shotgun on himself and aimed at where the problem was."

Phil Celmer III generally agrees with his mother. He was the last family member to visit Trapper when he and his new bride came to Jupiter on his college spring break in April 1968. "He walked and acted like an old man," says Celmer. "He cooked my wife and me some steaks that he'd especially driven to town for, but he only ate some fruit because the meat would 'sour my stomach.'

"He was too proud to tell me he had a catheter up his penis, but you could tell he was in great discomfort. He reminded me of my grandfather, who went from being a robust man to a guy who had congestive heart failure so bad at age 65 he couldn't even turn a screwdriver. He [Trapper] just wasn't enjoying life anymore. All the people he trusted were gone. He'd watched his friend Captain Frank die of throat cancer and my grandfather die of heart problems. And I don't think he had a clue as to what he'd do even if he did land that big sale."

Adds Celmer: "I don't think the thought of death was all that horrible to him. He had put down hundreds of badly wounded animals, and now he knew he was one of them."

And yet....

Both Bessie and John DuBois had lingering doubts as long as they lived. "The people at the inquest were just trying to fit the thing to make it a suicide," she told the *Palm Beach Post* in 1975. "There have been rumors...astounding ones. Sometimes I wonder." [18]

VII Restoration & Rebirth

1968 –

Sylvia Pennock left Trapper's camp intact when she visited with her boyfriend in August 1968. But others would not. Whereas the remote location was once Trapper's best protection against intruders, it was now an inviting target because it was so difficult for local police or park rangers to patrol. With no one to step out from behind a tree and call "Who goes there?" the site was fair game for teenage beer parties, souvenir seekers and those who were convinced Trapper had buried a treasure somewhere on the property.

During the week after his body was found, 350 traps disappeared, along with all the hides and skins he'd been curing. Soon people were arriving in pickup trucks and loading up cords from the massive woodpile.

Ed Gluckler, a *Stuart News* reporter and member of the Jonathan Dickinson State Park Advisory Board, visited the site in the fall of 1968 and found the inside of the guest cabin a "shambles." The refrigerator had been cannibalized, the stove overturned and wooden cabinets yanked from the wall and splintered on the floor. Bunk beds had been toppled, sheets and blankets stripped away and the mattresses ripped open in a frantic search for hidden money. The floor was thick with broken glass and wooden debris, including a wooden sign that said:

PLEASE LEAVE THIS CABIN CLEAN AS YOU CAN

Outside, the gas-driven pump that had once operated the ingenious water system had been torn away from its shed beneath the concrete cistern. Two of the rental rowboats had been sunk and the third was missing. Across the river a wheelbarrow was upside down and half underwater. Trapper had bought it new that summer.

By year-end the camp looked somewhere between a combat zone and a hurricane devastation scene. The three-car garage had been burned to the ground. Craters in the sand remained where valuable coconut palms had been uprooted and carted off. Other holes and mounds of dirt were all about where people had dug for treasure. What was left of the garden and fruit trees had browned for lack of irrigation. And everywhere was a layer of beer cans, bottles, Kentucky Fried Chicken boxes and spent shotgun shells.

The only good to come from the vandalism is that it galvanized outraged conservationists and hastened the complicated land deal Trapper had been negotiating from Bessie DuBois' pay phone. Thanks to Bill Lund, who was president of the Izaak Walton League of Florida and determined to preserve the Trapper Nelson legend, the state Game and Fresh Water Fish Commission was persuaded to station a team of rangers as guards until the state park could get the proper authority to do the job itself.

Ironically, Trapper himself had been the biggest barrier to
the deal that would have transferred his land to the state, even
though it would have granted him lifetime occupancy of the
100 acres surrounding his riverside residence. Because the
War Department had never compensated him or the DuBois
family after requisitioning their Kitching Creek plots, he distrusted the state as well and haggled endlessly over details
(oil and gas rights, for example). But now Trapper was removed from the equation and an enticing alternative offer
had appeared on the horizon.

Here was the new deal. Lost Tree Village in North Palm
Beach was fast becoming one of Florida's most successful
upscale golfing communities. Its developers now had their
eyes on 360 acres of state park frontage along U.S. Route 1
in northern Tequesta. Their proposition: Would the Florida
Department of Recreation and Parks be interested in swapping the state park land even up if they (the developers)
shelled out the cash to buy Trapper Nelson's 857 acres and
added it to the southwest section of the park?

To Bill Lund and the Izaak Walton League, the answer was
obvious. Same for the state's persistent and patient Charlie
Smith, who had wooed the cagey Trapper for so long. The
land along U.S. Route 1 was undistinguished and under-
used. Trapper's land would not only gain the park an extra
497 acres, it would preserve the Loxahatchee from further
development and preserve the home of local legend for visitors to appreciate. Moreover, both properties were appraised
at nearly the same value: Nelson's land at $1,329,125 and the
smaller state park section (but seven miles nearer the ocean)
at $1,306,000.

For the Philip Celmer family and two sisters in Trenton —
the only heirs to his estate — it represented a quick cash deal

and more money than they'd ever seen. The last barrier was the governor's cabinet, which met on January 28, 1969. At a crucial point in the presentation, Governor Claude Kirk turned to Bill Lund in the audience and said, "All I want to know is, will this protect the Loxahatchee River?"

"It sure is a major step," Lund replied.

And with that the governor and cabinet approved the purchase. "It's the greatest day I ever had in my life," a beaming Lund told reporters afterward.

Although the 360-acre state tract was of scant interest to state park managers, its undulating dunes spelled idyllic sand traps and rolling fairway to the developers. Once work crews had picked up the thousands of spent rifle shells embedded in the sand from Camp Murphy days, they built the posh Jupiter Hills Club, known today as one the nation's premiere golf courses.

Just before the proceeds of Vince Nelson's estate were to be divided by his heirs, lawyers showed up representing his "widow." Yes, one Lucille Gee Nelson Howard, age 54, resident of Juno Beach, claimed her share of the joint property she owned with her husband of so many years.

Estate lawyers quickly noted that Widow Gee had no case because she relinquished all claims to Trapper's property when she accepted a $40,000 settlement on proceeds from the 215 acres Trapper sold in 1964. Yet, she still walked off with a $5,000 nuisance fee because to litigate her claim would have meant interminable delays before the anxious heirs got any money.

It was not until September 4, 1977 that the damage to Trapper Nelson's camp was sufficiently restored to open it again to visitors. And then it would be only on weekends. The park lacked the money to provide adequate ranger staffing.

It still does.

On April 11, 1984, Park rangers Robert Schuh and Karin Nelms were in the midst of replacing the cement between the logs in what had been Trapper's main cabin. Part of the job involved re-chinking the walls around the fireplace, an area that had never been reconstructed.

"As I worked, I knocked a small hole out where the wall meets the fireplace and I guess just instinctively reached my hand in," says Schuh." He pulled it out and said to Nelms, "Maybe you want to have a look at this."

"And there he was holding all this dirty money," she said. "It was unbelievable."

Trapper hadn't buried all those coins from the boat tourists and army poker pigeons in his pineapple patch after all. He'd done the most convenient thing available. He'd walked over to the fireplace and deposited them, so to speak, in his own cement piggy bank.

The stash included silver dollars and coins ranging from 1890 all the way up to 1964. In all there were 5,005 coins totaling $1,829.46. Today, thanks to the honesty of two park rangers, they reside in the state archives in Tallahassee.

Those who want to visit Trapper Nelson's today can take one or two approaches.

First, you can launch a canoe or kayak in the upper part of the Loxahatchee during the early morning hours. Just look for the canoe put-in signs on Indiantown Road 1.4 miles west of the I-95 and Florida Turnpike interchanges. The current will take you downstream about five miles, under a canopy of venerable cypress and to the Trapper Nelson dock just in time for a picnic lunch (no food is sold at the site). If you lack your own kayak or canoe, you can rent one near the put-in spot from Canoe Outfitters of Florida. Call owner Eric Bailey at 561/746-7053.

Second, you can take your own powerboat upriver (idle speed only) or rent a canoe at Jonathan Dickinson State Park. Enter on u.s. Route 1 (16450 s.e. Federal Highway) and drive to the riverfront concession building. Paddling against the current can be a bit much for some, so be aware that you can also make the trip to Trapper's on the *Loxahatchee Queen II*, the park's 44-seat, covered pontoon boat. The guided tours leave at 9:00, 11:00, 1:00 and 3:00. Jonathan Dickinson State Park River Tours can be reached at 772/746-1466.

Epilogue
The Suitcase in the Attic

Throughout the research on this book, the people who best helped me grasp the Trapper Nelson persona were his nephew's wife, Lucille Celmer (now of Tavernier, Florida) and her son Phil III ("Flip" of boyhood) in Waretown, New Jersey. During one interview Phil said he just knew that somewhere the family had stashed a box of "papers" on Vince Nelson they'd been given after the funeral.

Perhaps, but after a while I could wait no longer. By early December 2001 I had just about finished the book manuscript when the phone rang and Phil was at the other end. "Guess what?" he said. "I was up in the attic looking for a box of Christmas decorations, and there in the back was an old suitcase."

The mother lode. The treasure of Tutankhamen! At that point I had relied mostly on media scraps and personal interviews, learning in the process how greatly personal recollections varied among people now in their seventies and eighties. When was Trapper born? 1909 was the consensus. What was his original name? Vincent Nostokovich, a Russian name. When did he come to Jupiter? Consensus: 1928 or '29. When did he move upstream? Sometime just before the war. Etcetera. A couple of days later I had two fat Express Mail boxes crammed with mortgage deeds, 45 letters in Trapper's own hand, family photos, more clips about Charlie's murder trial, Trapper's will, Social Security application, birth certificate, army papers — even an inventory of his safety deposit box at time of death. Bonus: a bunch of old 16mm family movies that had been converted to a videocassette.

There it was, enabling me to set a hundred details straight. Examples: Trapper was supposedly sent to some nameless army camp in Texas. Yet, his leg operation was done at an air force hospital in Keesler Field, Mississippi. Instead of knowing only that he married Lucille Gee "sometime during the war" (as everybody said), I now knew just when they got married and when Trapper filed his jerrybuilt divorce papers. And until then, because I'd never had a newspaper account of the final day of Charlie's murder trial, I had all but sent him off to jail with a jaunty wave and cocky swagger. Now came the missing piece showing how he had crumbled on the stand and told the real story.

The suitcase contents also raised some new questions I wasn't sure I wanted at such a late stage in the game (manuscripts are like children; you love them, but you're happy to see them out the door when their time comes). One example of a newly presented problem was a Photostat of a feature on Trapper Nelson that appeared in the *Miami Herald* of August 23, 1985. Amidst the usual garbled Nelson yarns were three paragraphs I'd never read before. Quoth one William Matuza, then 48, of Miami Beach: "I spent seven years of my boyhood living with Trapper in the 1950s. When I knew him he was in magnificent shape. We lived just like it was 100 years ago."

Wait a minute. Seven *years* and not one of the people interviewed for this book ever mentions a William Matuza?

Trapper, he continued, paid him $10 a week. "We had to feed all these animals in the zoo, and so we had lots of shooting. He had stolen all this ammunition from the army camp and buried it, then dug it up after the war. We always had plenty of ammunition" (and, if it included dynamite, would explain the goat episode and how Trapper toppled those big trees that fell across the river after 1960).

Matuza said he eventually left to live in Miami Beach, but returned unannounced in the mid-sixties in hopes of a visit for old time's sake. "He was fat and had a beard," said Trapper's apparent apprentice. "He just told me to get out. He said I now belonged to Miami Beach. I left and never saw him again. I think he started getting a little crazy. In the end, he was a nasty, nasty man — amazing but nasty."

Matuza, the fellow who supposedly lived with Nelson for seven years, would now be in his sixties. All attempts to locate a man by that name or get locals to remember him were fruitless until it dawned on me to ask Phil Celmer. He queried his mother and she said, "Oh sure. Matuza was a son of Trapper's second youngest sister, Emily. They called him Billy the Kid. He had come down with his brother Lefty to stay with Trapper in the summers. But the two of them were always getting into trouble. One time Trapper accused Billy of stealing and told his sister not to let them come down anymore. And that's probably why Emily and her family never got into the will."

Louis Freeman remembers Billy the Kid, and not too favorably, either. "I remember one case where he broke into a museum stole a bronze bell from *The Republic* (an oil tanker sunk during World War II) and sold it for scrap. Another time he was arrested for stealing material from a building that that been blown apart by a hurricane. None of it was ever condoned by Trapper Nelson."

So, Trapper had teenage troubles from *within* and without.

Alas, none of the treasure trove shed any light on Charlie Nelson, the man who had the most motive for murder. The only scrap of new information is a yellowed single page written on July 23, 1939 to "Sis" in Trenton. It comes from highway construction Camp #44 in Crystal River, Florida and thanks her for a money order. But other cards she sent, Charlie adds, were lost because she hadn't put the name Nelson on each and every one of them.

"We are finishing this road in a short while and will be moving to another road job in some different part of the state and will give you the change of address as soon as possible," the letter states.

He signs it "Your Loving Brother, Chuck." And with that he fades from recorded history.

The biggest mystery of all remains the nature of Trapper's death. Murder, accident or suicide? When I began researching this book I had no opinion whatever, save perhaps a subliminal hope that I'd discover something sensational that would sell books. Since the suitcase contents arrived, I can only say that I am led away from suicide and from accidental death by circumstantial evidence and the opinions of people I respect. The personal papers and few letters that were written by Vince Nelson in the late sixties indicate:

First, a man who still loved trapping and living on his "ranch," as he called it in later life. On February 20, 1968, when some were describing him as old and ailing, Trapper wrote Phil Jr. "Am thankful I have been able to complete another winter trapping and hunting season without any trouble on my line." Although he now finds "many boats on the stream," the people are "now leaving me alone." His words indicate contentment.

Second, a man whose letters were largely logical and thoughtful, with no trace of paranoia. True, he thought developers and lawyers were connivers and distrusted some of his neighbors. But how would you feel if you were walking along the riverside and saw a squatter busily fencing off 50 acres of your property? Trapper had done so, and maybe his suspicions were framed by similar episodes.

Third, writing in his late fifties, Trapper seemed placidly accepting of old age and deteriorating health. The February 20, 1968 letter notes that "as you get older you find that time is moving a lot faster and that you had better get your pleasures while there is still time left." Yes, he's had a hernia that kept him from chopping wood for weeks, but it's on the mend and he'll soon be able to resume. He has "gas trouble," because "my digestive system is slowing down." But by "giving up eating fat animals" [such as raccoon and possum] he's going to alleviate the problem. He also mentions dieting at least twice, and once losing 15 pounds. One wonders, do suicidal people bother to diet so they can look and feel better?

Fourth, the probate record belies a popular notion that Trapper had slipped into serious tax trouble again and took the shotgun as a way to end the stress of it all. He wrote glowingly of new businesses entering Jupiter, rising waterfront values and new roads being built through western properties. He looked to getting "around $1 million" for his land and figured that if he retained oil and gas rights, "it could be worth another million in 20 or 30 years." Do suicidal people worry about oil and gas rights many years away?

Probate records show that Trapper had no reason to hurry

a deal as he had in 1964. The official court tally showed $2,000 cash in hundreds and twenties in a safe deposit box, $57,500 at Community Federal Savings & Loan, a $10,000 C D at the same S & L, $9,400 at First National Bank of Stuart, $1,980 at First Federal S & L and $250 in an Indiantown bank. Against that roughly $81,000 in cash, the biggest debts he owed were $341 to an attorney, $60 to a rental storage company and $43.98 to Joe Vleck at Oceanview Service for fixing the jeep. There's no mention of any tax arrears.

So...did he or didn't he? To help you further judge for yourself, I've included some representative letters in the following appendix. They show a man who was mostly logical but sometimes prejudiced, mostly noble but sometimes petty, mostly thoughtful but sometimes impulsive, depending on how he felt and who threatened his peace of mind. In short, he was in many respects a lot like the rest of us. And on that basis, he shouldn't have taken his life because a couple of body parts were malfunctioning.

But then again, Vince Nelson was a unique individual with his own recipe for living — and perhaps for dying. Dave Brooker, who visited Trapper often as a teenager, and then often daily as a tour boat captain, put it this way: "I guess I knew him about as well as anyone. But then I really didn't know him."

And that is why Trapper Nelson remains the Legend of the Loxahatchee.

Appendix

Letters from Trapper Nelson

1951 – 68

Here is some representative correspondence — and excerpts — sent by Vince Nelson to members of his family in Trenton, New Jersey during the period 1951-1968. For a man with huge hands and little formal education, Trapper's handwriting is remarkably deft and clear. Because each letter was invariably one long paragraph, I have indented from time to time to make reading easier. However, I have left intact Trapper's pet misspellings on grounds that they make up part of his personality.

Bear in mind that he writes to or writes about three relatives named Phil:

- Philip Celmer Sr., husband of his sister Marcie, and his senior by ten years.
- Philip Celmer Jr., son of the above and Trapper's nephew. Married to Lucille. Eventually one of three heirs to Trapper's estate.
- Philip Celmer III (called "Flip" in boyhood), son of Phil Jr. and Lucille. Grandnephew of Trapper, who was already 37 when he was born.

July 12, 1951

Dear Phil [Sr.]:

I now have the agreement to buy the land so please have your bank transfer $2,000 to me at the Citizens Bank in Stuart. I will use my own money for the remainder, as the price is $2,500 for 95 acres. The lot plus 40 acres west of it.

I trapped 2 wildcats on the 4th and the other one has healed up well. Will sell them this week to the same party that bought the others. The mosquitoes became bad this morning as we've had rain daily since you left. The hot water works well and everyone likes it. Am getting guests each weekend. Will close with luck to all. Keep after young Phil on the invention.
— Vince

August 21, 1951

Dear Phil [Sr.]:

[An excerpt from one of only two letters in the collection that Trapper wrote on a typewriter] I finished the fireplace this morning and placed a concrete cap on top of four blocks on end. Its 18 feet high and looks good. I will dismantle the scaffold to-day and be ready for the wall to-morrow. Have been eating pineapples now for over a month and soon will be through with them for the year. I have a good crop of citrus this year and hope the hurricanes lay off for the next 6 weeks as one passed through south of florida a few days ago and hit in mexico. I captured 2 wildcats last week and a rattlesnake. The bugs are thinning out now as the northeast winds are starting to blow now. Will close with best wishes to all, Vince.

Nov. 3, 1951

Dear Marcie:

[Also typewritten.] Received your letter and was very sorry to hear that [sisters] Connie and Nellie are having health troubles. My back which bothered me for four months has been well for over a month. I started reducing and lost 15 pounds which makes a lot of difference. Am working a little each day on my cabin and now am filling in the walls as the roof has been finished a couple of weeks ago. The roof is built much stronger than any of the others and should survive any hurricane. There were no blows here this season so have a large crop of fruit and will ship you some in December as its still green. Have been trapping for over a month and am getting plenty of game and have finally fattened all of my alligators including the two new ones eight and seven feet long.

Fur prices are dropping so will not spend too much time trapping but will keep working on the cabin as I have about two months more work remaining on it. My project for [her husband] Phil will be to put in the plumbing and running water in my cabin same as that in the guest cabin and am starting to gather the necessary material. I will put in the cess poll myself to save time and have that ready. Have had a few guests recently and all like the cabin now that its all modern. Have just finished breakfast of fried rabbit and fresh biscuits. Am eating well now on good game as the woods are at the best now although the fishing is poor but I don't have time to fish now. Am hoping we get some cool weather so I can sell some firewood as I have 11 cords stacked for sale. I received the magazine on orchids and find it has a lot of good information. Some of my orchids are now in bloom and will sell some as soon as people start to come out as it is too early as yet. Give my regards to Phil and the family. — Vince.

Sept. 24, 1952

Hello, Marcie: Received two letters from you and believe you were wise not to sell, as the waterfront property will be worth a thousand or more per acre in five years. Tell Phil not to answer any letters from real estate men as there are 300 in the Palm Beach area and most of them are crooks and confidence men who will beat him out of money in some manner. The line about homes for old people is all baloney, as most old People live in trailers and there is at least 30 miles of waterfront property for sale in the Jupiter area.

I will be looking forward to seeing you and the family in November and believe you will really enjoy a winter vacation as there will be no bugs and the fishing is usually very good at that time. Am planting and cutting wood now for exercise but expect to start work on a pump house soon. Yesterday I moved a large mango tree in front of the guest cabin.

[He discusses the deed to the property the Celmers purchased the year before.]

There has been little rain and no hurricanes as yet and the hurricane season is almost over. My orange crop is good so you will be down in time for lots of fruit. Bring along some of the old baskets and you will be able to take some home. Will close with regards to all. — Vince.

August 17, 1955

Hello Marcie: The weather is as yet perfect and no rain since you left. Fishing is swell. Tell Phil I caught a 5 lb. bass and 3 smaller ones on live bait in our special fishing hole. Also caught a turtle in the trap I set in the goat pasture. Am busy finishing off many small jobs as the rainy season is due any day. Am enclosing your letter and the mortgage [to the Celmer property] which has been recorded in Stuart.

Am starting top plant pineapples [handwriting garbled] and will set out a few trees before the rainy season comes in. You must have felt Hurricane Connie. It did not come in close enough to be noticed here. My lemons are coming in now and guava too. [He closes by advising Phil to make a notation on his property deed that he is retaining oil and gas leasing rights.]

May 2, 1958

Hello Marcie: Was glad to hear that you are over your cold. I had a bad one 2 months ago. You sure missed having some good bass. I am eating lots of fish, mostly bass. The weather is sunny and warm now. Pratt & Whitney is ready to build their $42 million plant. This will be a big deal and should raise values on property in the Jupiter area. Am enclosing a page of the Harbor Isles [newspaper ad]. This is just ½ mile past your land and Tequesta is ½ mile nearer to Jupiter but on the same road. In other words, you are between these 2 sub divisions. Write in to them and ask for a brochure on the Isles and this will show you where your property lies. I drove Phil to this area and showed him around. Will close with luck to all. — Vince.

I caught 9 bass today. Some were big ones.

July 21, 1958

Hello Marcie: Received your letter and note from the realtor. I believe someone is interested in your property and is trying to find out how anxious you are to sell. The area there is beginning to develop and you have a block which could make 120 lots of large size. The adjoining property has been surveyed so you can now see your property line on the north.

I am surveying some of my river property and have a chance to get 30 acres of waterfront from the state. It will cost me plenty but I must get it now before conditions change here. I will need most or all of your Stuart account [a savings account he had persuaded the Celmers to set up on grounds that Florida institutions paid higher interest rates] to handle this transaction and will give you a 5% mortgage for security [½ point more than the s & l's were paying]. Don't [decrease?] your account by any withdrawals without letting me know first as I have 2 blank checks which Phil signed and I don't want them to bounce. Jupiter is growing fast but large acreage plots have slowed down, but the prices are not dropping. A year from now you will see some real development and higher prices.

Weather has been fine and am getting lots of good fishing. Am working on my dock now. Am doing better now than in the winter as the cold weather slowed down my business. Am getting too many booze parties but am taking steps to thin them out. Give my regards to the family. — Vince.

Nov. 17, 1958

Hello Marcie: Received your clipping [perhaps a public notice in the newspaper] which is important as it means my neighbor a Mr. Hoyt is trying to get to the river around my property. He can make his 900-acre ranch a waterfront subdivision if he gets this trade. He could bring the canal from the Loxahatchee into his ranch. He wants to subdivide and wants to buy me out now but I want to wait at least one more year. Have notified people who will try to stop him for personal reasons. I will not try to stop him as he is too big for me to handle. He gave me a trapping-hunting-fishing lease on 160 acres of his ranch. It takes in Cypress Creek where the fishing is good. Am trying to borrow some money from him on a mortgage for three years. If I do I will form a corporation and will hire someone to manage it for me. Am willing to try Bill [?] if he will take orders and no boozing, as this is now a serious business here. Lots of drunks and teenagers to control. Will furnish transportation and a good wage. Am not ready as yet but will let him know when I am ready.

I will deduct $1,000 from your account today to repay my taxes and give my lawyer a retainer. My tax was $640 — it doubled 3 years in a row. Paid a surveyor $1500.00 last month so your bank account won't last long. Am clearing all my titles now which will cost plenty and may do some speculating so will need plenty of money. Don't talk about big money in front of the kids as it will cause us all lots of grief. Values around Jupiter have doubled in the last year and the town has started to boom. 2 lawyers, 2 doctors, 1 dentist, 1 bank are here now. Apartments are now going upp and lots of cheap housing. At least one new developer each 2 weeks or so.

Have started a full trap line and now have plenty of good hunting and fishing. Will go over to the North Fork this week to look around. They should be tarring the road by your 40 acres by now. It won't belong now and I will be able to move your 40 acres for a real figure. Will close with luck. — Vince

---

Feb. 23, 1960

Hello Marcie: Am getting along well and am now busy as the tourist season is at full capacity. The cruise runs every day and I also get many drive inns. The old bridge was rebuilt with new lumber yesterday. Fishing is good and last week I caught an 8 lb. bass at my dock.

I am still working on my park deal [an effort to buy, not sell]. However I hired a new engineer and he will get a good lawyer. I can gain about 50 acres of low ground all waterfront. Its now expensive for me to do anything as the lawyers and engineers are out to get all they can. I still have a couple of thousand left. It is getting expensive to borrow money on mortgages as they now get 10% [interest] on undeveloped land. I believe I can get by for another year without borrowing any more. From now on I will find it necessary to keep at least one lawyer and engineer on the payroll also a surveyor. Since property values have gone upp I must protect my interests.

A tar road will be built along your 40 acres on the N. Fork soon as the money has been appropriated. There are two sub divisions past your acreage but no buildings on them as yet. They are Harbor Isles [and] Iroquois Park. Your property is worth about $3,000 per acre now. If you get any inquiries let me know about it as the sharp operators will be after you. [Before closing he mentions some locals who, in his opinion, sold too cheaply.]

April 2, 1960

Hello Phil [Sr.]: Just a few lines to let you know all is well out here. Fishing is good and so is my hunting.

You now have a tar road along your property and it runs into Harbor Isle past your place. There is an 80-acre sub-division alongside of your 40 acres. However, there is no building on either as yet. Your property is now worth about $4,000 per acre. That's what Painter & Co. is now asking for the adjoining property. Jupiter is now growing faster all the time. You will see much more development when you come down this summer.

I have been looking for offers from big developers for my ranch as I won't be able to hold it much longer. Too many problems and rising taxes and insurance will make it a bad risk for me now. Some undeveloped acreage in Palm Beach county is taxed at $20 per acre although most of it at $5 - $8 per acre. Martin [County] will raise its taxes again this year.

I believe there is oil here in Florida, so I will withhold the royalty on ½ [of the property] I sell. I have now fired Crory and now have a Jupiter lawyer. It is difficult to find an honest lawyer. It seems that I have too much temptation for them and they try to take me for a sucker. Will close with luck. — Vince.

Sept. 8, 1960
Hello Phil:

The rainy season has been on for the past two weeks with rain daily. The creeks are flooded and poor fishing, but the hunting is good and am preparing for another trapping season.

Have closed my camp to all the public including the cruise. Now I feel a lot safer as it was a real risk in many ways dealing with the public. Will now trap and farm for a loss. Have tried to sell some of my property including your 40 [acres] in 10 are tracts but found no buyers. High tax valuations have stopped all buying except where developers can use the land immediately. I can't pay the coming taxes in November so will mortgage a large portion of my property. Will pay 10% interest but that's the best I can do. However, I can get a 4 year loan and by then I hope to be able to sell. The mortgage will not prevent me from selling the property. If all turns out well I will have plenty of cash in a couple of days. I will set aside enough to take care of mortgage [payments] and taxes and expenses and will have some left over to re-invest in land.

I would like to buy your 40 acres for $100,000 with $10,000 down payment and the balance of $90,000 carried at 4% interest for 12 years. [He then calculates how much the Celmers will earn each year from his interest payments. The last page of the letter is missing.]

Oct. 3, 1960

[Vince Nelson now has his $100,000 loan and owes the Celmers their $10,000 cash down payment on the 40 acres he's bought from them on a 12 year mortgage. Now he encourages them to deposit the $10,000 in Florida and make it available to him for further land purchases. Determine for yourself whether or not he has their or his own self-interest uppermost in mind.]

Hello Marcie:

Am going to town today to see if my lawyer is ready with the mortgage and deed. He was getting the abstract upp today and also getting title insurance. The sellers customarily pay for this but I will pay it myself. It will cost about $1,000. You will receive a check for $10,000 which you should bank down here in Florida to get 4% interest. You will have to pay Federal income tax on the profit. You should discount all of the cost of the land — taxes — lawyer fees. Also you should file for half the income yourself to keep the tax down. You will need a tax consultant. The $90,000 mortgage is not taxable until you receive cash on it. Your interest on it will be $3,600 next year.

[He discusses other amounts he owes the Celmers for prior loans.] I can pay you and Phil this amount in another mortgage on another tract of land and you won't have any tax to pay on any of it. As long as Phil is working this would keep his income down and build up his equity, which would be drawing 4% each year. When he quits working he could then take cash each year.

I have the [$10,000] cash on deposit in Jupiter and Riveria Beach, so don't get nervous, as good mortgages are better and safer than savings banks. A steel rolling plant is coming into Lake Park soon. In a couple of years this area should be booming. Right now money is hard to get, but after the election it should be more plentiful. Don't let the family know you have any money as they will mooch it away from you. The rains have quit and the floods are subsiding now. Sincerely, Vince.

Jan. 3, 1961

Hello Marcie: Well, another year has come and I hope it turns out well. This is one year for me to look forward too as now I do not have to meet the public in a business capacity. It was a strain the last two years as the teenagers and kids gave me a rough time. I now have a firm control over my camp and have time to fish and trap leisurely.

Another bridge is being considered across the channel of the river about 5 miles below here and it does not have a draw, which will cut off large boats and future development barges, dredges, etc. Am trying to stop its construction as it is a poor cut rate deal which will lower property values above it. As bridge is needed but one with a draw which should be built by the state or county as it would cost too much for a small developer.

[The remainder of the letter discusses a problem that cropped up with the land he bought from the Celmers. Turns out that the property had a prior lien on it. They agree to pay a lawyer $800 to obtain free title.]

April 2, 1961

Spring is here now and the tourists are thinning out around town. Fishing is the besting several years as the salt water has backed upp to my camp. Lots of snook, bass, mullet. Have had my ranch surveyed and concrete markers set each 660' around the outside perimeter. I find that my neighbors were trying to steal by fencing about 50 acres of land. I will now move the fences they built to their proper places.

I bough 40 acres last week for $312 per acre. Real estate is beginning to sell again after a 2 year dormancy. I am anxious to sell some in order to get rid of a dangerous mortgage which a local man holds.

There is a chance that a high bridge will replace the original low one at Tequesta and if this happens I should expect developers will begin to develop the North Fork.

Am enjoying the camp now that the drunks and insolent teenagers are out. They had lots of trouble with some of them at Lauderdale. They were around my camp last year and were taking over and setting a bad example for the local teens.

Am having a big crop of mangoes this year because of dry weather. My lemon crop is blooming and I have more trees in fruit each year. The Spanish daggers Phil brought in from the beach are in bloom. My neighbor to the west has almost finished his canal to the Loxahatchee it is 6 ft below sea level. Will work on my fences which will completely encircle my ranch. I hope to be completed in a couple of months and will then start to pull upp most of my docks. Have had a lawyer contesting the fixed bridge across the Loxahatchee which would lower values of all my land by at least 50%. Best of luck — Vince.

Dec.4, 1961

Hello Marcie: Sorry to hear about Phil [who had been di-
agnosed with congestive heart failure]. I think your best bet
would be to come down to Jupiter with him as soon as he can
travel and rent an apartment on Indiantown Road for the winter. There are many small apartments within a few hundred
feet of the 5 and 10, Super Market, Greens Dry Goods and
now a doctor is next to Greens store. He hasn't much time
left, so he should quit work and spend the winter here in the
sunshine and eat oranges. Would do you good, too. There
are now many old people living in this area and no car is necessary as everything is within walking distance. I will pay you
all the interest and some principal next month which will be
more than you could possibly spend here. You could come
out to the camp each week for a barbecue as I have at least
one each week. You could buy a lot or two and built a winter
home in this area as there are many lots for sale but are being
bought off fast now as Jupiter is ready for a boom in 62.

I have a good orange and lemon crop now — more than I
can eat. Have pulled upp most of my dock and the people
are now leaving me alone. Will try to get some easy mortgage
money next month from John D. MacArthur (the big developer of Palm Beach Gardens, 20 square miles, and Lake Park
south of Jupiter). The RCA plant is in his development with
another factory going upp. I want to get rid of Offutt's tough
[$100,000 at 10%] mortgage as it could get me in trouble.
Disney is looking for a location to build a Disneyland in
Florida and is considering Lake Park or the Loxahatchee, so
I may be able to make a sale yet.

[He summarizes his active opposition to the low bridge
over the North Fork and laments spending $1,000 on lawyers

to appear before the State Park Board in protest.] I don't trust these state agencies as they too are crooked.

The low ground adjoining my highlands in Section 16 is still in the hands of my Fort Pierce lawyer and am going to carry the battle to the Supreme Court if necessary to get the adjoining 60 acres of land. The Park Board is after it but they have no legal authority to claim it. If you need a thousand or two just drop me a line and I can mail you a check as I have the money on deposit in Jupiter. The coldest temperature so far has been 55%. Would like to see some real cool weather. My trapline is keeping me busy and will continue til February. Will close with luck. — Vince.

Jan. 2, 1962
Hello Marcie: Another year has rolled by and this is the year I believe has much in store for me. Am busy trapping and hunting and do lots of wood chopping to keep warm as winter has finally come here. Temperatures dropped to 37 a couple of mornings. I like the cold weather as I find I can keep active most of the time. Will send you some orange blossom honey soon now that the Xmas [?] is over.

[The remainder of the letter discusses legal costs for clearing the title to the 45 acres the Celmers had purchased.]

Oct. 14, 1962
Hello Phil: I am enjoying my fall hunting and trapping. The summer heat is over and nights are getting cooler. I have lots of avocados and my citrus will soon be ripe. Jupiter is now getting a water plant which should start the town to growing. There are 3 churches being built and numerous business houses as well as a new higher bridge over the N. Fork. This will surely give me a chance to sell there.

I hope so as I cannot go much longer without borrowing again and getting in debt deeper. Am enclosing an agreement for you and Marcie to sign in front of a notary and one witness. [In essence, it calls for a moratorium on his principal and interest payments to the Celmers.] If I sell before the end of 1963 I will pick upp the mortgage. If I miss payment of interest or principal when due you can call for payment of the entire mortgage immediately. I'm not worried about you, but don't believe I can rely too much on Marcie. She either has bad advice or she does not realize that I am the one who has the worries as your mortgage is a good one for you and Marcie. I have had a few people interested but not enough to buy. [He discusses a nearby development that sold only 30 of 570 building lots during the year.] There are several houses for sale just a couple of hundred feet away from the [new] medical center priced at $20,000, as this is a swanky area. I caught a nice snook yesterday trolling. I put copper sheeting on the entire bottom of one of my inboards so now the worms will not be able to damage the bottom. Will close with luck. — Vince.

Oct. 30. 1962

Hello Phil: Received the moratorium [the notarized agreement allowing him to postpone payments on the Celmer mortgage], which should keep me from going broke until I can sell. I'm sure trying now and this season may get me out of the hole.

Am putting out my winter trapline and am chopping wood to keep in shape. It's a mistake to relax too much as I put on too much weight. My citrus will be ripe in about 2 weeks. Don't have any time to work on The Hill [an Indian mound he had discovered on his property and was excavating for artifacts] as I hurt my hip and this gives me some trouble as yet but it will pass over soon I hope. A big builder has come into the town of Jupiter to build 70 water front homes. Jupiter now has city water and a larger Post Office will soon be built. Will close with luck. — Vince.

Dec. 10, 1962

Hello Phil: I sent you some more avocados and will send more if they arrive well. If frozen or stolen get a report of it from the delivery man and send it to me as I can collect damages. I have more fruit than I can eat.

My trapline is doing well enough. Caught a fox and 2 rabbits this morning. I speared 44 mullets big ones on Thanksgiving enough to last me a month. The fireplace is really something swell. I get upp at 4 A.M. to sit around waiting for daylight to run my line.

It won't be long now — 2 or 3 years — and the county will all be opened and hunting and trapping ruined. Am having trouble with trespassers and dogs (a sign of civilization). I think a big rocket plant is coming soon west of Jupiter this would bring in the builders as no one buys land to set and wait as its too high now.

You should come down for a couple weeks with Marcie and [their younger sister] Connie. She could help Marcie and she can drive a car. Also all dental assistants [Connie presumably being one] are trained to nursing and handling of patients so she would know how to help you in case of trouble. You are not getting any younger and Marcie did not look good on her last visit. I can't leave as I have too many people to watch. A new neighbor bough and is now developing the 100 acres where the power line crosses the river. He wants to move the power line and onto my property and ruin my property.

[He next discusses a court's dismissal of a suit he had filed and speculates that he was "double crossed" by his lawyer. He then mentions a notice in the *Stuart News* announcing foreclosure on a $108,000 mortgage located in the same area as the Celmer-Nelson property.] There are lots of foreclosures, but some, I believe, are phony where directors [of a corporation] buy back the land for themselves and trick investors. Nonlisted corporations are poor places [in which] to put money, as its easy to steal it legally. Have been offered Royal American stock for the ranch [by developer John MacArthur]. I believe MacArthur is trying to buy upp all the land in this area. He has his own corporation of $100,000,000. He is building Palm Beach Gardens and will eventually extend it to Jupiter and maybe here if he doesn't go broke first. He is also president of Bankers Life and Casualty Insurance Co. of Chicago. It's a half billion dollar company.

The bridge across the N. Fork is not completed as yet. I will pay your interest after the first of Jan. by depositing it to your account at Jupiter and it will be earning 4 1/4 from the first of the month. [The remainder discusses more details of amounts he owes the Celmers.]

December 31, 1962

Hello Phil: I hope your battery rig works well. It's something I never heard off. I lost 10 lbs and now weigh 236 as the trap line gives me about 3 hours workout daily and then I chop and saw wood. My fireplace is a life saver and I usually get up at 4 or 5 o'clock to sit around it before going out on the line, which is producing plenty of game, The frost did not harm my fruit and will send you some more if they lift this embargo.

Let me know if it's okay to send you a mortgage for the

$3,620 which I will owe you as interest to date. You won't pay taxes on it until you receive the cash. You will have to pay taxes on the interest earned on your savings account even if you do not receive it but let it ride.

MacArthur is buying land in Martin County now near my area, so I may be able to sell him some as I will be broke in the fall as I will meet a $5,080 payment in March and September and that party will foreclose if I miss my 30 days. I think I will be able to sell some this winter now that the holidays are about over for the season. Will close with luck. - Vince

---

Jan. 14, 1963

Hello Marcie: I was sorry to hear that Phil's pacemaker did not correct his [blowouts?]. You know the doctors do the best they can and sometimes one thing works and on most people and fails on a few. This business of getting old is no joke. There are many things that I cannot do now. I ruptured myself in two places finishing my pavilion a few years ago and realized it was time to quit. Maybe Phil should have quit two years ago when I bought his property. I designed the deal especially for him so he could retire.

I am doing well on my trap line. My leg is now well and I can start more digging at the hill [Indian mound] when I'm not too busy cutting wood. I sell firewood and have sold plenty of it this winter, which is not over yet. My avocados frosted off the trees, but all of my citrus is o.k. as I have a little shelter here from the swamp.

I deposited $620 to your account Jan. 10 last week and will make out a mortgage to both of you for the balance of $3,000. This bank in Jupiter pays 4 1/4 % on the quarter and is a good investment. I keep most of my money there, which I don't need for current expenses. I have a check account in N. Palm Beach also have a safety deposit box there to keep all of my mortgages and deeds as the camp is no longer safe. Too many crooks around Jupiter now. The N. Fork Bridge is finished and should be able to get an offer for some of my property. Am trying to sell part of my ranch to Macarthur of Palm Beach Gardens. He is the largest developer on the east coast. The business outlook is good , so if I sell I'll pick up the small mortgages as I will not sell any Small tracts as I could lose my tax status if I sold four parcels. Am waiting for one big deal and I expect 1963 will be my year.

Give my regards to Phil and let's hope the doctors figure out his problem. Will send you some sweet fruit if they lift the embargo. Will close with lots of luck. — Vince.

Feb. 15, 1963

Dear Phil: [Letter addressed to him as patient in University of Pennsylvania Hospital.] Received a couple of letters from Marcie with all the news about your condition. Did you get the mortgage of $3,000 which I sent to you recently? [Actually, it was an installment note to extend payments on his purchase of the Celmers' 45 acres.] You had better get well and come to Florida before the summer heat gets here. I have lots of sweet fruit rotting as I cannot eat it all. The cold did not hurt any fruit in Martin County. Remember the coconut tree which grew so fast along my woodpile? I just picked upp 10 coconuts which fell from it — all ripe. That's 2 trees now with nuts. My trapping is good and so are the fur prices. I trapped 5 wildcats last week — a record and have 4 otters in a cage.

Jupiter is now building a larger Post Office and another bank is going upp soon. The town now has city water and fire hydrants and lots of new stores and a medical center will be completed in a week or two.2 doctors, 2 dentists.

John B. MacArthur the developer of Palm Beach Gardens is now my neighbor and now borders my ranch to the south on a mile front. He now owns 60,000 acres which stretch from Lake Park to here about 12 miles. His latest buy was 4,000 acres and this ties into my ranch. I'm sure he wants to get to the river, so may be able to sell some land soon. He's the 6th richest man in the country and he wants to build a town of 100,000 people in the next ten years. He is bringing in plants into his town and has a RCA plant now which employs 900 people with a larger one coming to make appliances. It looks as though his Palm Beach Gardens will reach the Loxahatchee River in time.

I dug some this morning into the Hill and am now 60 feet into it [he seems to be using the fertile shellrock in the Indian mound as planting soil]. Am planting avocados and pineapples in the reclaimed land as I have too many oranges now. Will close with lots of luck. — Vince.

[Trapper wrote Phil another letter on Feb. 28. Like the previous one, it was full of encouraging news about Jupiter's development and reasons why Phil and Marcie should rent a place there quickly. In mid-March 1963 he received word that Phil Sr. had died during an operation to repair a heart valve and install a new pacemaker.]

March 24, 1963

Dear Marcie: So now you are a rich widow. You won't have any trouble getting along as long as your money holds out. That you will learn real quick as everyone will want to get some of your money pr advise you how to spend it.

You were very foolish in transferring your money from

Jupiter as it was earning you 4 1/4 [interest] quarterly. The banks upp north pay only 3% and that only on the half year or yearly. You lost several hundreds of dollars by not waiting to the end of the quarter. You are acting like a child when you think that you pulled anything over on the bank as I told them and they make reports too the government of all accounts. What you need is a financial advisor but I no longer count as the moochers in Trenton will clean you out soon enough.

[He explains that his sister won't owe federal taxes because the land was joint property.] Keep away from the lawyers as they will rob you for sure. Crory in Stuart [the attorney he "fired"] gave me bad advice which cost me lots of money, so I learned not to trust lawyers. Would advise you to start a checking account with a small deposit not over $500 so you won't need to carry cash around or you may get robbed if you keep cash around. Will write to you next week as soon as I find out the score from the Jupiter bank. Jupiter opened another bank last month. — Vince.

Aug.5, 1963

[This is the first recorded letter in which Trapper writes to Phil Jr., the son of Phil Sr. and Marcie. He and his widowed mother are upset because the mortgages signed by Trapper for the 45 acres he bought from them appear to designate only Phil Sr. as seller. This could snarl this and other notes by Trapper in probate court. Trapper replies.]

Hello Phil: Received your letter of the 29th July. Again I must stress the fact that you do not need a lawyer. The county judge can furnish all of the necessary information at no cost and the rates are set by the Internal Revenue and state tax bodies. A letter to them will bring you all the information you will need to handle the matter.

Of course if you appear to be too lazy to handle your own money others will soon relieve you of it. [He adds that it's all speculative anyway, because the land purchase note he gave the Celmers can't be collected until he has first paid off his $100,000 loan to Offutt.] If I fail to raise it by September 1964 the money lenders could take over all of my property as well as my bank accounts.

Would suggest you come down with Flip [Phil III] and the other boy for business consultation — also to see this property and find out the right course to take if I fail to make good. I have been trying to figure out how to get you down here to study the problem without the interference of your family. Unless you learn to keep your family out of your business you soon won't have any. It would take about five or six days to cover all the angles and see what the potential of the property is, and I'm sure it could be a business expense as there is no other way for me to acquaint you with all the problems — and believe me there are plenty of them.

My ranch is now fenced and the gate is locked about one mile out from my cabins. This has finally been effective in keeping out the local people. The people who are welcome have keys. [Since there is no close or signature, a page or two may be missing.]

[During the traumatic year leading up to the decision on the courthouse steps to sell his 215 acres to Bessemer, there are no letters from Trapper in his family's records. The only indicator of the family tensions existing then is the letter from Phil Celmer Jr. to Trapper cited on page 77. Then, some two

months after the transaction has been settled and cash proceeds disbursed, Trapper writes his nephew again.]

June 17, 1965
Hello Phil: Received the mortgages note and check last
week and the figures seem o.k. For the first time in 20 years
I'm free of debt. The bridge across the Loxahatchee is completed and the Islands are being raised by an 18-inch dredge.
The roads are not as yet completed across the river but should
be soon. The county will carry a road across the bridges west-
ward to the Turnpike, thence north to the Hobe Sound grade.
This will go along my south boundary of the ranch and will
open the area west of the Park. Food Fair and Publix are now
almost completed on the north side by the river in Jupiter.
Community Fed. Savings & Loan is going to move to a new
location next to where the Bowling Lane used to be and the
Lanes went bankrupt and are now a restaurant.

[After further reports of burgeoning development in Jupiter,
he writes:] I bought a new truck as the old one was in bad
shape (a 1960), Has your company failed as yet? You should
be well off for a long time now if the tax people don't get too
much, I'll have to figure my tax soon and will have to pay on
the money Offutt loaned me as that will become part of my
profit. Will close with luck. — Vince.

Sept. 10, 1967
Hello Phil: [The letter to his nephew begins with a glowing description of building activity in Tequesta and plans for
a new county road across the river.] It will create a demand
for property on the water in Martin County. Bessemer and
MacArthur are now trying to buy upp property on the river
but are keeping their plans secret to hold down prices. There
are a number of acreage tracts on the river which they will

try to get before the public is aware of their intentions. A golf course and a clubhouse could cost about 1 ½ million however plenty of money is available for the big outfits! Last month the old man [MacArthur] bough a motel on Miami Beach for 4.7million, so he isn't short on money. He's also buying land along the Intracoastal north of Juno.

Miller, the director of the State Parks, sent a man down to see me recently in regard to getting my property in Section 20. He was not prepared to make any offer as yet. So it looks like the coming winter may produce a big deal. The syndicates to the west and south have not acted on any of my offers.

My tax bill of $27,000 was settled last month for 12,000 and six percent. My [?] was O.K. and I was worried that some of the big guys might buy him upp to break me. Bessemer tried to take over 10,000 acres from Irons as the 2 yr time was upp but I had [his attorney] Rogers file a suit against the bank naming them co-defendant and asked for a court ruling. Also I signed a suit against Michael Phipps as president of Bessemer, this suit being held for use if it became necessary to use. Phipps is another Offutt, so now I know where I stand with him. Any deal with Bessemer will be a hard deal now for them. You can't trust any of the big people as MacArthur has tried to cheat me on stock deals to get my property. The only way to deal with people like that is all cash.

The nervous tension which has been the major cause of all of my stomach trouble has left me now and the gas by itself does not bother me much now. Tense stomach muscles were pressing around my bladder and caused my difficulty, as the gas was not able to get by and cut me off. Am waiting now for a new trapping season and may start to increase my line next month if it gets cool early as I think it will. Have cut lots of wood this past summer and am still eating ripe pineapples as they came in late. Also I have 3 trees loaded with avocados. Will close with best of health and luck. — Vince.

Feb. 20, 1968

Hello Phil [his nephew]: So you finally decided to take a vacation. You know as you get older you find that time is moving a lot faster and you had better get your pleasures while there is till some time left. Am thankful that I have been able to complete another winter trapping and hunting season without any trouble on my line. There are now many boats on the stream, but the people have been leaving me alone. The kinds that used to give me trouble are now married or in the services so that got them off my back. I managed to get several deer, which is more than I can ever use now as I am eating less meat which seems to be part of my gas trouble. My digestive action is now slowing down so now I have quit eating fat animals — coon — opossum — this is the trouble all old people face as they get older.

Temperature in the mornings has been in the lower 50s or upper 40s for the past two weeks, as winter did not get here until the last month. However furs are no longer prime and have pulled upp my long line. The fireplace is burning day and night and lots of wood has been used upp. The hot water set upp for showers is a life saver as I could not take a cold shower now in cool weather.

The building pace in Tequesta and Jupiter is now moving at a fast pace trying to beat inflation. I have several cash offers now but none as yet acceptable. Last week at the Tequesta weekly coffee meeting Reed from Jupiter Island took positive steps to raise 1 million to save the Loxahatchee from developers. Foundations will be asked to cover a local contribution of $2000. This sum can be doubled [?] by foundations which will bring it up to $256,000 then the state will double this to ½ million, then the Federal govt will double to 1 million which will be enough. I have about 515 acres in Sec. 16-20 which the state wants. There are about 4 other tracts they will need, but my property is the key. If they don't try to get tough with me they can have my property at fair value. So far no commitments from me to any. I expect to retain the royalty on ½ gas and oil and [?] of mineral on all of my future sales. This won't cost me anything but could be worth a million in 20 or 30 years.

I [?] stop at one of the stores on Tequesta Drive and get some steak-corn-baked potatoes and drive west to your father's property then cross the river. The road across the river has been in use for about 2 months and this is now bringing in speculators. I am now only five miles from the banks in Tequesta. Will close with best of luck and health. — Vince.

[Undated letter, probably in March 1968]

Hello Phil: My trapping is now in high gear, and trapped 3 large coon this morning. Prices are expected to be lower owing to unsettled business conditions however the line is now a hobby and the Revenue Service will not accept much of a write off. Not enough volume of business. My taxes were the same as last year but should rise next year as now the road has been built across the upper river and this will increase land values on the west side of the river. You will not need to go to Jupiter to get to my place now, but turn west on Tequesta Drive for 3 miles then cross over the river [today's Island Way bridge].

[After more glowing news of development in Tequesta, Trapper mentions a mutual friend named "Tony" who drove out to visit him.] He looks well for his 55 years. I'm 59 now and am wondering how it slipped up on me.

The State Park is now definitely taking steps to make me an offer for my ranch. Ocean frontage is being bought as well as wooded ranch lands all over the state.

The weather is unusually warm so far, the lowest about 55% and most nighs in the lower sixties. The fur has not primed as yet but will grade NO.2. The woodpile keeps getting larger all the time as I cut some wood each evening. I have plenty of fruit but eat very little of it as I still have a gas problem with my stomach. I think that I eat too much, so now I will try some fasting to see if there is any change. I whipped the nervous tension by taking a couple of highballs in the evening or some wine before going to bed.

Tequesta now has 3 doctors and 3 dentists and this town should grow larger than Jupiter as it now has a 5 story high rise on the island and a 3 story is being built. There is 4 miles of ocean frontage which will be annexed to Tequesta. In 1946 Histead tried to sell the town of Jupiter ½ mile of ocean frontage for $35 per foot. Bessemer acquired his property in a mortgage loan and recently sold 1000 feet for $385 per foot.

Am enclosing a key [to his entrance gate] if you get down. Best of luck and health. — Vince.

June 2, 1968

[This is the last letter in the Celmer family collection and was written around seven weeks before Trapper's death. Unfortunately, most of it contained lighthearted chitchat. Phil Celmer Jr. had taken up flying and Trapper takes two pages telling him about a friend who also flies, about a book he read by an Alaskan bush pilot, about another article on flying in

the May *Outdoor Life*, and a feature on Eddie Rickenbacker
he'd read in *Time*. Nothing about sickness or suffering.]

The building in this Tequesta area is speeding upp to beat
inflation. The Hunt Club is being offered at ½ million with
several offers $50,000 short as yet. I haven't seen the Out-
door Recreation [state park representative] since his offer of
$1,000 [per acre?] some months ago. Tallahassee is on verge
of a civil war with the politicians fighting each other. Our
Governor, a republican has a Democratic house and Senate
and they won't cooperate on anything so politics is at a stand-
still. The governor uses his veto powers too much. Each new
election should produce more republicans to back him upp.

MacArthur bough the Allstate tract (2100 acres) which is
on my South boundary for ½ mile. He offered a building and
dock for use as a shark factory in Riveria Beach. There were
3 cases of sharks mauling swimmers in the past 2 months so
the county will subsidize a shark factory to reduce the number of sharks. This plant should handle 250 each week. It
has been operating in Ft. Pierce but will move [something
missing] on a subsidy guarantee. Shark livers are no longer
used, as a synthetic has taken its place and hides have
dropped in price. The meat is frozen and sells in Europe,
Will close with luck. — Vince.

And so end the letters from Vince Nelson and our only opportunity to learn firsthand just how or what may have compelled him to take his own life in late July 1968. Instead, our
only glimpse is of a man who calmly accepts growing older
and is even optimistic about overcoming his aches and pains.
Judging from the amount of space taken up by land values,

he seems to be absorbed, above all, in a dramatic poker game in which he, a Polish peasant's son, with just a little more staying power, will wrest from the cleverest of lawyers and developers a million dollar stake *plus* the right to remain on his beloved Loxahatchee for life.

Trapper in the late 1960s. The last published photo before his death at age 59. (FLORIDA HISTORY CENTER & MUSEUM)

Endnotes

One of an author's most delicate tasks is to document one's sources properly while not burdening the reader with endless, needless distractions. The latter surely would happen had I footnoted each statement about Trapper Nelson and life in early Jupiter. Hence, I have taken a shortcut. In the preceding text, a quote in the present tense almost always comes from a personal author interview. When it appears in past tense (e.g., he said, she wrote), the quote was drawn from media accounts or *The Loxahatchee Lament* — the latter a precious anthology of early memories published by the *Jupiter Courier* in 1978. The 18 endnotes below rated special attention, in my opinion.

1. Until now it's been commonly agreed that Vince Nelson was born in 1909. Press accounts have listed his original name as Nostokovich, although some surviving family members remember it as Nontokevitch. The confusion surrounding the name isn't difficult to explain

in that busy immigration officials on Ellis Island commonly "Americanized" names they heard phonetically from new arrivals who often couldn't read or write themselves. And in this instance, the matter was complicated by the fact that the family's native town of Vilna had been fought over by Russia and Poland in the years following World War I.

Recently, an enterprising volunteer researcher for Jonathan Dickinson State Park decided to see if the Social Security Administration (SSA) could shed any light on the matter. After all, if Trapper Nelson had a mercantile mind and read the *Wall Street Journal* (which certainly covered news of the growing Social Security system) he'd be sure not to miss out on getting some benefits to help him in his old age. So, the volunteer wrote the SSA in 2000 under the Freedom of Information Act, inquiring whether a Vincent Nelson from Jupiter, Florida had ever applied for a Social Security number.

Sure enough, Vincent Nelson had filed an application on November 9, 1962. Where the form asked for date of birth, he had written November 6, 1908. Mother's maiden name? "Unknown," he wrote. Father's name? *Casmier Natulkiewicz.*

Yet, could even the son, hindered by limited schooling, have garbled the family name just as an immigration official might have done? The researcher needed a second opinion. He (or she) again wrote the SSA asking if it had any applications on file from anyone named Natulkiewicz in Trenton, New Jersey.

Bingo again! Registered in the system was one Nellie Natulkiewicz (since deceased), born July 28, 1906, to

Casmier Natulkiewicz. Nellie was Vince's second oldest sister and one of his summer visitors. She also knew her mother's maiden name: Patinski.

2. *Palm Beach Post*, January 7, 1932, p.1.

3. *The Loxahatchee Lament.* Jupiter: Cary Publications Inc., 1978. Pages 167-68 quote an article by Harold Rolls from the March 1, 1923, *Palm Beach Post.*

4. *Palm Beach Post-Times*, March 12, 1972, p. C1.

5. DuBois, Bessie Wilson, *The History of the Loxahatchee River.* Jupiter: Self-published, 1981. p. 24.

6. *The Loxahatchee Lament*, p. 160.

7. Nathaniel P. Reed of Jupiter Island has headed his family's real estate and hotel businesses in Florida for most of his life. However, he has had almost concurrent careers in government service and conservation. Reed served under six Florida governors and two presidents, including terms as chairman of the Florida Department of Air and Water Pollution Control, and Assistant Secretary of the U.S. Department of the Interior for Fish, Wildlife and Parks. He also helped form 1000 Friends of Florida and chaired a governor's commission whose recommendations led to the creation of Preservation 2000, the nation's most ambitious state land acquisition and preservation program (now Florida Forever).

8. *The History of the Loxahatchee River*, p. 29.

9. Judge Chillingworth had decided to seek disbarment
   of a local attorney, Joseph Alexander Peel, for running
   a Bolita (numbers) racket up in the Hispanic and "col-
   ored" sections of West Palm Beach when the latter got
   wind of it and prevailed on a couple of Riviera Beach
   toughs to abduct the judge and his wife at gunpoint.

   Just before dawn one night in June 1954 the two gun-
   men forced the dazed couple — still in their bedclothes
   — from their beachfront home in Manalapan and
   slammed them into a waiting motorboat. As the boat
   headed out in the calm sea, the desperate couple offered
   their unknown kidnappers $100,000 just to leave them
   alone. But to no avail. They manacled Midge Chillingworth and pushed her overboard. When the frantic
   judge dove over the side in a hopeless effort to untan-
   gle her, they speared him with a gaff hook and then
   crushed his skull with hammer blows.

   The bodies were never found. The truth came to light
   almost by accident. Richard J. Procyk, now retired in
   Jupiter (see p. 99), was in his first year as a Miami Beach
   detective in 1959 when he arrested one Floyd "Lucky"
   Holzapfel in a hotel jewel heist. After questioning some
   of his cronies, they learned that Holzapfel had gotten
   drunk one night and bragged about "taking care of a
   judge and his wife." This led to a "sting" in which another drinking party was staged — this time in a bugged
   room in which "Lucky" told the story in gruesome de-
   tail as the police recorded every word.

   Postscript: The relationship between Judge Curtis
   Chillingworth and Vince Nelson piques the imagina-
   tion but only leads up blind alleys. Both Chillingworth
   and Nelson were known to be avid competitors for land

subject to delinquent tax sales. No paper trail exists to explain precisely how Nelson acquired most of his 857 acres on the west side of the Loxahatchee. The probate inventory of Nelson's safe deposit box at death (but not furnishing details on each document) includes a "receipt from C.E. Chillingworth, dated Oct. 19, 1949, for $1,000 in cash and Western Union draft for $3,000." Other papers involve a quit-claim deed issued to Nelson by the executors of Chillingworth's estate and a "warranty deed — Chillingworth to Nelson." Finally, the inventory lists an envelope postmarked June 7, 1949, "enclosing certain correspondence from C. E. Chillingworth to Nelson." None of the individual records has been found to date.

10. The probate inventory of Vince Nelson's safe deposit box at death revealed papers showing that Lucile Gee had married one Harold B. Larzelere Jr. on April 12, 1936 and that she married Edward Edgar Kingsbury on November 25, 1947. Presumably after successive divorces from husbands Larzelere, Nelson and Kingsbury, she wed a man surnamed Howard in Juno Beach.

11. *Palm Beach Post*, August 6, 1998, p. E1.

12. *Jupiter Courier*, Letter to the Editor, August 11, 1978, p.6.

13. *Palm Beach Post*, Letter to the Editor, September 22, 1998, p. 19A.

14. Ibid. March 12, 1972.

15. *Requiem*, by Robert Louis Stevenson (1850-1894).

16. *Palm Beach Post-Times*, March 12, 1972, p. C10.

17. Despite the absence of any documents that someone named "Alphonzo Capone" actually owned land in west Jupiter, local residents insist convincingly that a getaway spot was indeed owned in the well-camouflaged name of a mob functionary. Ruby Fortner Lanier, for one, notes that in 1924, when she was twelve, her father was hired as a foreman of an experimental agricultural farm. It was located in what is today's Jupiter Farms, "just south-west of the [actor] Burt Reynolds spread."

Adds Ms. Lanier: "There were only three or four houses out our way and we all knew that one of them belonged to some famous outlaw. That's all we knew. After I was married, my husband [Elzie Lanier] liked to hunt. One day he was out back of this 'outlaw' place and the man he was with said 'Elzie, I've just unearthed a skeleton.' Elzie said, 'It must be some animal.' He said, 'No, this is a human.' And pretty soon they had dug up three or four skeletons. I just know they were pretty scared and didn't say much about it."

18. *Palm Beach Post*, 1975 (Month and day unknown).

About the Cover

The illustration on the front cover is a reproduction of a 1997 watercolor of Trapper Nelson's boat shed by artist Ron Parvu. As he explains it:

> "After what seems like an eternity, moving up-river through a tropical ecosystem, the first sign of man's intrusion is Trapper's old boat shed. An intrusion to be sure, but a welcomed sight to those who felt lost in this jungle paradise."

This is one of Ron Parvu's many portraits of the people, places and wildlife that make the Loxahatchee a uniquely wild and scenic river. Raised in northeastern Ohio, Parvu now lives and paints in Tequesta, Florida, where his many one-man shows have won wide acclaim. For originals or limited print editions, contact:

Loxahatchee River Gallery
450 Dover Road, Tequesta, Florida 33469.
Phone: 561-744-1298
online: www.watercolor-artist.com/.

About the Author

Author James D. Snyder and wife Sue live on the Loxahatchee River near the border of Jonathan Dickinson State Park and a mile or so from Trapper Nelson's camp (as the crow flies). As avid kayakers, the park and its historical centerpiece have been a big part of the their lives since moving to Jupiter in 1992.

The author, who majored in journalism at Northwestern University and received a graduate degree in political science from The George Washington University, spent most of his writing career in the nation's capital as editor and publisher of newsmagazines on business and medicine. He has also written widely for such diverse publications as *Parade, Smithsonian* and *Harvard Business Review*.

Other books by James D. Snyder:

All God's Children, an historical novel about the intertwined fates of the Christians, Romans and Jews of the first century (1999, 680 pp., ISBN 0-9675200-0-2).

The Faith and the Power, a history of the earliest Christians in the turbulent first 40 years after the crucifixion, and how they confronted the Roman Empire in the darkest days of its debauchery (2002, 416 pp. ISBN 0-9675200-2-9).